HOW TO G

The Right

BUSINESS
SCHOOL

MW00677324

HOW TO GET INTO

The Right
BUSINESS
SCHOOL

James L. Strachan, Ph.D., C.M.A.

VGM Career Horizons
NTC/Contemporary Publishing Group

Library of Congress Cataloging-in-Publication Data

Strachan, James L.
    How to get into the right business school / James L. Strachan.—
2nd ed.
       p.   cm. — (How to get into —)
  Includes bibliographical references (p.).
    ISBN 0-8442-6453-9
    1. Business schools—United States—Handbooks, manuals, etc.
2. College choice—United States—Handbooks, manuals, etc.
3. Master of business administration degree—United States—
Handbooks, manuals, etc.   I. Title. II. Series.
HF1131.S86   1998
650'.071' 173—dc21   98-26008
                                                      CIP

Published by VGM Career Horizons
A division of NTC/Contemporary Publishing Group, Inc.
4255 West Touhy Avenue, Lincolnwood (Chicago), Illinois 60646-1975 U.S.A.
Copyright © 1995, 1999 by NTC/Contemporary Publishing Group, Inc.
All rights reserved. No part of this book may be reproduced, stored in a retrieval
system, or transmitted in any form or by any means, electronic, mechanical,
photocopying, recording, or otherwise, without the prior permission of
NTC/Contemporary Publishing Group, Inc.
Printed in the United States of America
International Standard Book Number: 0-8442-6453-9

99 00 01 02 03 04 CU 18 17 16 15 14 13 12 11 10 9 8 7 6 5 4 3 2 1

To Marcia, Mitchell, Nicole, and Tara, who add sunlight to
my life each and every day

Contents

Acknowledgments

The objective of this book is to provide the highest possible quality of reference. The process of writing this book began with the knowledge and experience of Terri Justofin, former Director of Admissions for the MBA program at the Weatherhead School of Management at Case Western Reserve University. This revision has the added expertise of Nancy Roth Remington, Director of International Programs of the Goizueta Business School at Emory University. Nancy contributed her knowledge and experience by editing the manuscript and writing the chapter "Focus On International Applicants," which enhances the value of this new edition by making it even more useful to the growing number of foreign students seeking an MBA. In addition, we must thank Julie Barefoot, who scrutinized the entire manuscript and made valuable suggestions, many of which are reflected in the final text.

Other colleagues—Andrea Hershatter, Patrick Noonan, and Sarah Smith of the Goizueta Business School and Charles Becker of the Economics Institute in Boulder, Colorado—have been equally generous with their time and advice, lending their particular expertise to individual chapters, especially the new chapter focusing on international applicants.

Finally, the contributions of Mike Bissler, Laura Garrett, Gita Gulati, and Dan Moodie, in addition to many others who must remain unnamed, are recognized and appreciated. A special and sincere thank you to each of you. You are indeed professionals of the highest standards.

Jim Strachan
Nancy Roth Remington

Introduction

It is the objective of this book to enhance your MBA application process by impressing upon you the following:

- There are steps and actions that can be taken that will enhance your chances of being selected into the graduate program of your choice. You have an obligation to yourself to undertake those steps and actions.

- Focused and guided preparation can help you to efficiently improve your performance on the GMAT (Graduate Management Admissions Test), which will, in turn, increase the likelihood of your being accepted by the graduate school of your choice. For the international student, this same focused and guided preparation is also required to achieve the requisite TOEFL performance.

- Focused and guided evaluation of your own background can help you write essays that more accurately reflect the many positive qualities you will bring to the MBA program of your choice.

- It is the prerogative of those involved in the admissions process to decide who will and who will not be accepted into their program; therefore, do not make a decision for them by deciding not to apply to a given program because of your doubts of being accepted. To apply is your job; making the admission decision is theirs.

- You should be realistic in your evaluation of programs and your "fit" within those programs. However, remember that persuasive essays and strong recommendation letters can significantly enhance the likelihood of your being admitted to your top choices.

- It may well be that following the guidance provided in this book will cause you to learn more about yourself than you could have imagined.

Who Am I? What Am I About?

- Do I have the intellectual ability and the desire to complete graduate-level study in an MBA program?

- Am I willing to make the commitment necessary to successfully complete that program?

- Am I the type of person who would be a positive addition to that program?

- Am I willing to be an active participant in that program?

- Do I see myself as one who will reflect positively upon that program after its completion?

If your answer to all of these questions is an honest, emphatic "YES!" then this book is for you.

Why a Book About Business School Applications?

Over the many years that I have served on the MBA admissions committee for a highly rated private university, I have observed two aspects of the application process that need to be conveyed to individuals currently involved in that process. The first is that the process has become more extensive and challenging, a change that must be respected in order to prepare a successful application. The second is that both my colleagues and I have recommended for acceptance applicants who, based on their GMAT (Graduate Management Admissions Test) scores and/or grade-point averages, did not appear "qualified." We did so because there was something in each person's application that strongly conveyed that he or she was unique, could meet the demands of the program, was someone we wanted to have in the program, and would positively reflect on the program after graduation. (Conversely, there have been applicants that might have been accepted but were not because they did not project this same feeling of excitement.) The effective demonstration of strong communication skills, strong leadership skills, high motivation, the ability to think creatively, and particular combinations of these qualities were deemed to compensate for low grades or GMAT scores. Guiding you through the application process and through projecting your uniqueness and excitement is one significant purpose of this book.

This book also addresses applicants' misconceptions about themselves as they relate to the application process. Numerous observations of and conversations with potential business school applicants suggest that many underestimate their ability to get into schools of their choice. Reasons for this underestimation include poor undergraduate grade-point averages, low GMAT scores, and poor personal perceptions of themselves. For now, be advised that there are strategies that can be employed and steps that can be taken to minimize the impact of perceived problems and perhaps even allow these factors to be used to your advantage. To do this, however, you must firmly believe in yourself and have both the willingness and the ability to convey that belief.

This book will help you maximize your chance of submitting a successful application to those business schools you view as being the best for you. It will help you understand the applications process, taking away some of its mystique. It will help you emphasize the "unique" you that must be conveyed throughout the application process. It will address the process of dedicated, objective, personal evaluation, which is a critical and inherent part of the application process.

Who Should Use This Book?

This book is designed to be used as a strategic reference for gaining admission to MBA programs in the United States. This book is equally valuable for U.S. and international applicants as they target MBA programs of interest to them and apply to them. If you are just beginning the process, then this book will help you by providing valuable guidance on how to evaluate programs and maximize your performance on the GMAT. If you are at the application stage of the process, then this book will provide guidelines intended to dramatically enhance your chances of submitting a successful application to your schools of choice.

This book does not purport to be an informational guide to MBA programs. It should not be used as either a career decision-making tool or as an aid in deciding whether the MBA degree should be pursued. There are many resources you should consult before reaching the decision to pursue the MBA. Where applicable, specific resources are cited on the many matters that will be of importance to you as you advance through the various stages of the application process.

If you have made the personal commitment to get your MBA, and you are now attempting to gain acceptance to the school(s) of your choice, then this book is designed for you.

The Right
BUSINESS
SCHOOL

1

There Is an MBA for You

The most important point in this chapter is made in the title. Regardless of your present situation, if you want an MBA degree, there is an MBA program in your future. The task at hand is to convince you that you are capable of being accepted into an MBA program that is right for you, a task that should not be that difficult given that you believe in yourself enough to have taken the initiative to obtain this book.

Don't Make Decisions for the Admissions Committee

It is important to understand and believe that there is no such creature as an "ideal" or "perfect" applicant. Attempting to compare yourself to this mythical creature will likely cause you to view yourself as being unqualified for many programs of interest and keep you from applying. By deciding not to apply, you are rejecting yourself rather than giving an admissions committee the chance to make a decision about you. Why make that decision for admissions committee members? That is their prerogative, not yours. Recognize that admissions committee members will, when asked, generally admit that "they do not know what they are looking for but believe that they will know it when they see it." If this is the case, how can you anticipate their perceptions of your application? So, if you believe that you are the type of person a particular program should and would want, submit your application and let those in charge decide whether to offer you admission.

A common misconception among prospective MBAs is that magical predetermined formulas exist for admission to particular schools. In some cases this is true but in most cases it is not. In general, admissions committees are much more focused on admitting individuals who will challenge their faculty, provide synergy in the student-faculty and student-student interaction, and favorably reflect on the program after completion. Diversity among those students selected is a high priority for any MBA class. Admitted students will come from a wide variety of educational, experiential, and cultural backgrounds and will bring with them differing records of accomplishment. Accordingly, you are encouraged to review the most recent year's class profile to determine which schools might consider you, and those to which your application would be a stretch.

Regardless of your educational, experiential, and cultural classification, if you are truly interested in a particular program, have a record of achievement, firmly believe in your ability, and are capable of forcefully and effectively conveying your strengths and uniqueness, then apply. Each program will have a profile, but it will also have exceptions to that profile. Recognize that for every member who reflects that profile there will be others who do not.

There are no excuses for eliminating yourself from a program of interest. Only by applying and letting the committee know your qualifications will you have the opportunity to be accepted into those programs you have determined to be right for you. The application fee that you may have to pay for that opportunity is a small monetary risk for the chance to be admitted.

Consider yourself to be that ideal candidate. Recognize that you have the potential to gain acceptance to those schools that are right for you. Submit applications to each of them using the guidance provided by this book, the remainder of which is devoted to explaining in a practical and effective way the thoughts, approaches, and strategies that will enhance your chances of acceptance.

2

Understanding MBA Programs

You may feel that you know what an MBA program is all about and be tempted to skip this chapter. You are encouraged not to do so for several reasons. First, if you read this chapter, you may save yourself thousands of dollars. Second, understanding the premise on which an MBA is designed can provide you with a legitimate reason for wanting to earn an MBA, a reason you may be asked to produce as part of the application process. Third, understanding the intent and the structure of the MBA degree requirements will reduce your anxiety over how you can use the MBA to your benefit.

The Nature of MBA Programs

Attempting to provide you with the latest pertinent information on MBA programs is analogous to attempting to hit the proverbial moving target. It is easy to get the impression that every aspect of existing programs, from program content to student support services, is undergoing constant review. For example, this chapter makes distinctions between twenty-course (two-year) programs for nonbusiness undergraduates and ten- to fourteen-course (one-year) programs for those with undergraduate business degrees. The number of one-year programs is growing in the United States but now they are being offered to the nonbusiness undergraduate. Such programs can be found at Northwestern, the University of Cincinnati, and the University of Pittsburgh. Harvard has an eighteen-month program.

The one saving factor is that the wheels of change tend to move slowly throughout the educational environment, which means that major, earthshaking changes generally become reality only after people have had a chance to become used to them. Many changes were made in the early to mid-1990s and now it seems that program structures and content may be entering a period of stability.

An Overview of "Traditional" MBA Programs

MBA programs were traditionally designed for nonbusiness undergraduates. (What this implies for those with undergraduate business majors is addressed later in this section.) Liberal arts, fine arts, science, and engineering majors are highly sought after by all MBA programs because of the creativity, critical thinking, and/or technical ability characteristic of people with these majors. It is for this reason that most U.S. MBA programs require two years of study, the first year consisting of introductory business courses and the second consisting of a few required courses and a number of electives. Many schools include the following courses in the first year: accounting, finance, marketing, operations or production management, economics, statistics, computer applications and systems analysis, and human resource management. Each of these courses presumes no prior academic study of its topic.

Frequently included in the second year is a comprehensive, or capstone, course that is intended to integrate all of the areas studied into a case analysis framework. Courses in law or ethics are also frequently found in the second year. Faculty may deem particular areas, such as finance, economics, computer applications, human resource management, and so on, to be of sufficient importance to merit additional course work during the second year.

In summary, the traditional two-year, twenty-course MBA program varies from consisting of fourteen to fifteen required courses and five to six elective courses to approximately ten required and ten elective courses. You will not be placed in a course for which you do not have the appropriate background. If you have taken a particular course and feel that you have retained a significant level of knowledge in and understanding of its subject matter, such that your retaking the course would be an ineffective use of your time, then you should investigate the availability of a waiver exam. You can take comfort in the inherent strength of the MBA—it can take any individual with ability and commitment from any starting point and transform that individual into a professional in a given field.

Making This Structure Work for You

There are two distinct sets of implications for the structure of the MBA program, and this section is subdivided accordingly. If you were a nonbusiness undergraduate major, the first section addresses your needs. Those holding an undergraduate business degree can proceed immediately to the second section.

The Nonbusiness Major

Again, the generally required first-year courses are accounting, finance, marketing, operations management, economics, statistics, computer applications and systems analysis, and human resource management. Each of these courses is taught with the presumption of no formal, prior knowledge. Knowing this should be comforting to you—you will not be at a disadvantage relative to your peers when you begin the program.

Review again the topics that are studied in the first year of the program. Note the encompassing range of these topics, which is of utmost significance. Recognize that you will likely not have to make any decisions about which specialization courses to take until the beginning of your second year. During the first year, you will study all of the specialization areas your particular institution has to offer and you will obtain a feel for the faculty within each area of specialization. You will gain insight into which areas are of interest to you and which are not.

You will be able to discern which areas tap your inherent strengths and aptitudes and which do not.

The end result is that you will be in a position to use personal knowledge, not guesswork, to decide how to use your electives during the second year. Whatever perceptions you had when you started—for example, to specialize in marketing or finance—may be confirmed or challenged. Either way, the structure of the program will work in your favor.

The Undergraduate Business Major

When you read that the structure of the MBA program is designed for the nonbusiness undergraduate and then read the list of courses generally required during the first year, at least two questions should immediately come to mind: "What does this structure mean to me?" and "Why should I have to take these courses again?" This is where knowing the structure of the MBA program might save you thousands of dollars.

Each MBA program in which you are interested will have an established policy regarding the applicant who has an undergraduate business degree. Some will take the position that students must meet all their MBA requirements—a position that results in a two-year commitment.

Other schools retain the two-year base program of twenty courses but allow substitutions. One approach is to waive the required course and replace it with an elective in that same area of study. Another approach is to waive the requirement and substitute an elective requirement.

A third approach, one which enables you to save a great deal of money, is to request a true waiver of required courses. With such a waiver, the number of courses required to be completed and the time required to earn the degree are reduced. One method frequently employed requires you to take a proficiency examination in the subject area for which you want waiver consideration. If you pass this examination with a certain score, you earn the waiver. The second method utilizes the grade you earned in a previously completed equivalent course. If the grade earned equals or exceeds the established cutoff grade, generally at least a B, then the course is waived. It must be noted, however, that with the rapid change in course content and the reduced ability to recall subject matter with the passage of time, a time limitation for waiver permission usually is imposed. A limitation of three to five years after completing the course is not unusual. Further, differing (and usually shorter) limitations may exist for quantitative and technical courses than for more qualitative courses. Generally, the required twenty courses can be reduced to ten to fourteen, a number that can be completed in one year, saving one year's costs.

The subject of waivers raises a question: "How much is it worth to save a year of full-time study?" To answer this question, simply add one year's tuition and living costs to one year of foregone salary and subtract any income that might be earned through a summer internship. For example, assume that, based on the number of years of experience currently preferred by many graduate programs, your annual salary was $40,000 to $50,000, that tuition and living costs for one year were $20,000 to $30,000, and that your summer internship would pay $5,000, waiving a year of courses could easily save you between $55,000 and $75,000.

There are more than twenty universities that offer a one-year option, and this number appears to be growing. You owe it to yourself to at least examine your eligibility for a one-year program.

Implications for the Application

A point stressed here and throughout this book is that it is imperative that you be honest with yourself throughout the application process. Responding with what you think the committee wants to hear is not the way to approach any essay. Attempting to use this approach may cause you to overlook important legitimate reasons for pursuing the degree. Equally dangerous is the presumption that the admissions committee members know what they want. The essay should be written by your rules—what you believe—and not by those of the admissions committee. Play the game on your terms by being honest with yourself.

Many people have a strong tendency to underestimate themselves and to downplay the obvious. This section examines some issues that relate the application process to your undergraduate background.

Again, the concerns of the nonbusiness undergraduate are addressed first. Then we consider the concerns of the business major.

The Nonbusiness Undergraduate

Recall that the MBA is designed for the applicant with your background, so use your background to your benefit. Keep the opening comments about integrity in mind as you consider how to integrate your background into the application process.

One frequently asked essay question is "How will the MBA benefit you?" The natural tendency is to look for some grandiose answer, such as, at the extreme, "to initiate the first business on a colonized planet." Or you may feel obligated to respond by selecting an area of specialization within the program. Either of these responses is more than acceptable if true, but what if it is not?

Imagine that you have the requisite business experience. Given that you were a nonbusiness major, you have likely found that you only partially understand the business environment. You have picked up on some of the terminology, but business has a unique language and perspectives with which you are uncomfortable. This discomfort may be causing you to avoid participating in discussions because you do not fully understand the substance of the discussions or because you fear that you will use the incorrect terminology and appear stupid. Regardless of the reason, the "you" that is being portrayed is not the real "you" and all that you can contribute. These are legitimate reasons for entering an MBA program and worthy responses to an essay question.

Another possibility is that you only partially understand the language and do not understand the decision-making process. Imagine that at your business you have submitted an idea of tremendous merit that has been turned down. For the life of you, you cannot understand why. After all, the idea would make money (but perhaps not enough). Perhaps the idea involves greater risk than you perceive or than management is willing to accept. Perhaps the direction your idea would take the company in is incompatible with the future directions being considered by upper-level management. Regardless, the desire to better understand the decision-making process is a legitimate reason for pursuing an MBA. It will be relatively easy to write a convincing essay on how the MBA can contribute to your understanding of the decision-making process because of your experience at work.

Another reason for pursuing the MBA may relate to directions your life has taken compared to those you anticipated while an undergraduate. Imagine that you were fully committed to bettering humanity by performing in a social service capacity. In fact, you have done this and have done so quite successfully, but with this success has come the opportunity to move higher up the managerial ranks and further from the service-provision ranks. With each successful step your need to expand your knowledge of business increases. This situation provides fertile ground for a convincing essay.

Having opted to pursue an undergraduate degree that is not business-related can work to your benefit. Some programs prefer that you have this background, so, take advantage of it. State, stress, and demonstrate your creative thinking ability, your ability to think critically, and/or your ability to dissect and resolve complex issues and problems. Make your background work for you.

The Undergraduate Business Major

Why are you going to pursue an MBA? After all, you already have a business background. You know the language of business and you presumably understand the decision-making process. What can an MBA do for you that your current background and experience do not provide? Responding that you need to earn an MBA because many of your workplace colleagues have done so and you need to keep up with them, that you need it to be promoted, or that having it will enable you to earn more money may be true, but such responses are unlikely to earn you many points with the members of the admission committee. Look deeply within yourself. If you cannot find an inner response other than one of those mentioned, reevaluate your pursuit of the degree.

One justification for earning the MBA can be found in the inherent structure of undergraduate business degree programs. Some programs are general in nature and do not require specialization. An MBA can help you gain additional knowledge in your area of choice. Even if your undergraduate program required you to specialize, undergraduate-level study is limited. The MBA offers the opportunity to extend your knowledge. Alternatively, you may have chosen one area of specialization for undergraduate study and now want to move into another based on the directions your professional life is taking and based on knowledge you have gained about yourself since graduating. Should any of these reasons apply to you, then you had better be able to convincingly expound upon the reason in your essay, a topic covered in Chapters 7 and 8. Merely stating such reasons will, at best, give you only a minimal advantage.

Why the Emphasis on Work Experience?

Until the early 1980s, having the MBA was, from an employer's perspective, much more important than work experience. Within a span of a very few years, this perspective rapidly changed. Now experience is expected by many employers, and is required by many MBA programs. This is because one of the goals of an MBA program is to increase the likelihood of your placement upon completion. Also, work experience will generally mean a higher reentry salary for graduates. Placement rate and the average starting salary of graduates are used as measures of a program's worth. The higher these two measures are, the better the program appears, the greater the application pool, and the more selective the admissions process. (As will be demonstrated later, however, using average starting salaries to judge a program is a mistake.)

There are additional reasons for the experience requirement, the most obvious of which is the maturity factor. Also, if you are willing to give up the comfort of a steady job and reduce your standard of living for one or two years, then chances are high that you have thought long and hard about your decision to pursue an MBA, have concluded how you can utilize the degree to your best advantage, and are thus likely to be the committed, dedicated student desired for the program. Your experience can help you integrate the various components of the program and will offer you perspectives that relate to the issues being addressed in class. Your employment history will help the committee members evaluate you as an individual in terms of preferred characteristics. It behooves you to weave all of these characteristics into your application material in order to convince the committee members that you should be preferred.

Having said this, it now must be noted that the employment environment is changing. The MBA degree is no longer the "golden ticket" to high salaries and rapid promotions. No longer does the Fortune 500 company represent the great sponge that will soak up any and all graduates. No longer can the campus career center be presumed to be responsible for your placement. Instead, you will find it necessary to take charge of your own employment search, which will include solicitation of nontraditional (small, medium-sized, venture) firms. The campus placement services will continue to exert maximum effort on behalf of students, but the emphasis has shifted to their *supporting* your efforts; the final responsibilities rest on your shoulders, not theirs.

3

Selecting the Right Program for You

The application process requires a critical, objective, constructive evaluation of yourself in terms of what you want to accomplish in order to derive the maximum enjoyment of your life. The most significant question you have to address is what you want your life to be. What type of lifestyle do you want for yourself? What do you want to try to accomplish? What balance do you want to strike between your professional accomplishments and your personal accomplishments?

Answering these questions can be a challenging and difficult experience, especially given the fact that your goals and objectives will change over time. You can find story after story of unanticipated midlife career changes. Mobility in career directions is one of the features of the American economic system, but knowledge of this mobility cannot offset the uncertainty engrained in the question, "But what if I make the wrong decision today?" The response is, "You have to make a decision, so make that decision using the best information available, go for it, and don't look back."

The goal of this chapter is to help you address issues that are relevant to your decision-making process. Included are factors you must consider as you go through that process. Do not expect to find answers here. The answers must come from within you.

Your Professional Goals

What do you want your professional career to be? Are you really determined to achieve the presidency of a Fortune 500 company? Are you out to make millions as a Wall Street investments phenomenon? Are you committed to becoming a superstar in international business? Do you want to be a national and international traveler as a team member of a top consulting firm?

If your answer is an emphatic *yes* to any of these questions, then, playing the odds, your choices of programs must first focus on the top ten and then on the very strong regional universities. Your chances of being recruited into the most competitive professions in the most successful companies are quite high with an MBA from the top schools. If you attend a strong regional program, then you will need to reach a higher level of achievement, make stronger connections, and obtain stronger recommendations than you would at one of the top ten schools, but you can still make connections with the top firms.

Do you see yourself as a player in a particular region or even a particular city? In this instance, getting your MBA from one of the top-ranked schools will be helpful, but it may well be that you should more carefully consider a program with a very strong regional identity. The reason is that the graduates from that program will have a tendency to gravitate toward and eventually become major players in the economic centers of that region. Attending that program and getting to know them as classmates means that you will have made very important contacts.

In the end, your ability, your connections (now captured under the more commonly used term *network*), and your luck will open doors for you. However, the importance of the network created with your colleagues and alumni should not be underestimated. Review of the placement statistics of the schools in which you are interested, with a special emphasis on the companies that recruit on that campus, the number of hires by those companies, and the functional areas in which those hired were placed, will provide you with some insight into the nature and strength of the network as it currently exists.

Cost Decisions

How much time and how many dollars are you able and willing to invest in your MBA? A reasonable estimate of the cost of one year is in the range of at least $55,000 to $75,000 if you opt to go full-time. Given that the traditional U.S. program is two academic years in length, you are looking at an investment that will easily exceed $100,000 and will likely approach at least $125,000 in the major private programs. Besides the traditional (but generally limited) sources—savings that you have accumulated and financial help from that constant fountain of support, your parents—what are some of the options available to help you finance this large investment?

Basically, there are four options: scholarships, assistantships, loans, and part-time work. Loans and part-time work are probably familiar to you at this point in your life and will not be further discussed except to note that incurring $40,000 to $50,000 in loans for the top two-year private programs is not uncommon. To be sure that you understand the difference between scholarships and assistantships, however, these will be defined.

A *scholarship* covers all or some portion of tuition, does not require you to work in order to receive it, is nontaxable, and may require you to maintain a specified level of academic accomplishment (grade point). Some scholarships extend beyond tuition and include living expense allowances. Most scholarship requests are built into the admissions process and require you to simply check the appropriate box on the application form in order to be considered. It is suggested that you review each school's recruitment literature to understand the minimum standards, such as grade-point average and GMAT score, that are required for consideration. If this information is not provided, then inquire through the admissions office. Be forewarned that you may find it necessary to retake the GMAT in order to place yourself in the scholarship range. Also be forewarned that you should inquire into the school's policies regarding the manner in which second and subsequent GMAT scores are treated. Distinctions may or may not be made between your first and subsequent scores. Some programs will count only the initial score, some the highest, and some the average of your scores.

An *assistantship*, in contrast, requires that you perform some type of service, (that is, work), in return for a waiver of some or all of the tuition and for dollars that, importantly, are classified as wages. Note that because you must work for the benefits provided by an assistantship, those benefits are subject to income tax regulations. Any waiver of tuition is defined as taxable income and hence subject to withholding. The waiver of the high tuition of private schools, then, can create a high taxable income and therefore cause a large amount to be withheld and substantially reduce your take-home pay. Most assistantships are independently awarded by specific departments and are based on particular talents or skills that you demonstrate that meet the needs of the departments. Assistantships, therefore, may require a separate application and consideration process.

You must now be made aware of the reality of the financial situation. The perception in the United States is that earning an undergraduate degree is a necessity, and for this reason a well-established process is in place to financially support undergraduate education, with a large portion of this support being predicated on demonstration of financial need. In contrast, earning a graduate business degree is viewed as a luxury, so financial support is not presumed. Accordingly, some schools still allocate their support funds on the basis of need, others allocate on the basis of merit, and still others consider both need and merit. Regardless, the highly competitive MBA programs will be equally competitive in terms of awarding scholarships and assistantships, which means that you must make every effort to present your most impressive application package to vie for the limited financial support. The up-and-coming programs frequently offer substantial financial aid, particularly scholarships, to meritorious students as a means of attracting them away from the top programs and as a means of enhancing the quality of their own programs.

Generally, greater scholarship opportunities exist at the strong regional private schools, while the strong state schools generally offer more graduate assistantships. Additional considerations will likely be extended to selected applicants a program wants to attract. For a more detailed source of information, you may want to consider ordering *The Official Guide to Financing Your MBA*, published by the Graduate Management Admissions Council, if you are seriously considering a wide range of programs. Or confer with the admissions representatives of those programs in which you have a specific interest.

One alternative way of reducing your cost is available if you earned an undergraduate business degree. There are over twenty programs that offer you the opportunity to earn the MBA in one year, thus saving you time and significant ($55,000 to $75,000) money. You will find, however, that this opportunity is available at few of the top schools. This opportunity is more frequently found in the strong regional programs. You must consider whether the extra year required and the strength of the reputation of the degree is worth the extra time, effort, and cost typical of the top programs.

Another alternative is to enroll in a program on a part-time basis. When you do this, your cost will likely decrease rapidly for two reasons, both related to your employment status. The first is that your employer will likely have a tuition reimbursement plan and will also have at least a partial reimbursement plan for expenses for at least the cost of your books and perhaps even for mileage. You may be required to finance one semester's cost because employers customarily reimburse you for a completed semester rather than advance you the funds necessary to begin a semester. The second reason for the reduced cost is that you will continue to earn your salary and benefits. Should you consider this option, it is strongly suggested that you consult with your human resource representative to determine whether there are certain programs that are preferred by the company. You can also use this consultation to become knowledgeable about your company's reimbursement policy, because some companies limit reimbursement to state school tuition rates. At this time you can also determine if your firm requires documentation that your course work options are job-related (for tax purposes) and learn about any other applicable program guidelines and policies.

The part-time alternative is not, however, cost-free. You will pay a high personal toll, about which more is said in the final section of this chapter. For now, what is important is that you recognize that part-time study exists as an option.

If you are considering pursuing the MBA on a part-time basis, the viable programs will be limited to those confined to a specific geographical area. Therefore, this chapter will be only minimally helpful to you because you can get much of the information you need from the resources in that area. If, however, you are going to attend full-time and are seeking the best options for your investment, then read on.

The Problem with Using Starting Salaries as Indicators of Quality

One statistic reported by MBA programs—sometimes with pride and sometimes with trepidation—is the average starting salaries of their recent grads. If the number reported shows a healthy gain and is also higher than those of competitor schools, then a feeling of pride swells throughout the institution. However, if the numbers do not look strong, questions start getting asked and the mood tends to pale. Regardless, a widespread perception may develop that average starting salary reflects the quality of a program, at least in the eyes of the employment market.

There are two weaknesses in this perception. The most obvious relates to the major regions and types of positions in which schools tend to place their graduates. The top schools tend to place their graduates in high-cost areas; starting salaries would thus have a natural tendency to be higher. The East Coast, the West Coast, and Chicago are known as being high-cost locations; starting salaries thus reflect a cost-of-living difference. The second weakness resulting from a straightforward comparison—the experience factor—is more likely to be overlooked. If a person has worked for five years, received at least one and more likely two promotions, spent two years improving capabilities in an MBA program, and reentered the workforce, it is highly unlikely that he or she will accept an opportunity representing a pay cut (although it does happen to a small percentage of graduates, regardless of the program).

For the moment, assume that your starting salary after completing undergraduate school was $30,000 and that during your five years of work experience you earned merit increases averaging 6 percent and received two promotions at the end of your second and fourth years, each resulting in a $5,000 increase. Your base compensation would be roughly $51,000 at the time of enrollment in an MBA program. If you further assume that at a minimum your compensation would increase at the 6 percent rate during the two years you were in the program, then your anticipated salary upon completion would approximate $58,000. On this basis, starting salaries equaling or exceeding $65,000 do not seem out of the ordinary.

Further, note that there has been no allowance for regional cost-of-living differences. Note also that no consideration has been given to the differing types of jobs that might be pursued by graduates. If, for example, more graduates enter the manufacturing or the nonprofit sectors than enter the investment banking and consulting sectors, then the average starting salaries would likely be lower. Finally, note that the average starting salaries become much more a function of the number of years of work experience required before being accepted into the program than of the quality of the program.

What if you opt to enter a program with fewer than five years of work experience? What should your approach be? You should compare your projected salary at the end of an equivalent period of time on the job. Suppose, for example, that you opted to work two years, earning the same 6 percent merit increases on the same starting salary of $30,000 but leaving just before you received that first promotion. At the time you enrolled in the program, you would have been earning approximately $34,000. You then spend two years in the program and accept a job paying $45,000, a level of compensation that is not unrealistic given your fewer years of work experience. You continue to earn the same 6 percent increases for two years and then receive your first promotion, which earns you a $5,000 increase. At this point, your compensation level would approximate $55,000. Assuming that you worked just one more year, your salary would approximate $59,000. This number is $6,000 less than the $65,000 projected earlier, but it would not take much for the salaries of the two paths to equalize. For example, an initial reentry salary of $50,000, (a reasonable amount for those programs with average starting salaries of approximately $65,000), leaving the other assumptions unchanged, would produce the same $65,000 salary at the end of the same period of time. It is, however, your reentry salary of $45,000 that will be used to compute the average starting salaries of the graduates of your program. Yet at the end of the same period of time you could easily and realistically be at the same level of compensation.

This type of evaluation is far more useful than one simply comparing the average starting salaries of the various programs. The numbers tend to reflect a work experience component, a regional component, and an industry placement component more than they reflect the quality of a program.

Big City or Small City?

What type of surrounding environment do you want? Do you want to go to school in a big city or a university town? Part-time job opportunities and access to business executives await you every day in a big-city location. So too does access to the cultural and sports activities the major cities have to offer. On the other hand, these offerings may not matter to you because the demands of graduate study do not allow for the same level of social interaction found at the undergraduate level, so you may not be able to take advantage of them.

As a general rule, whether for programs or cities, larger size offers larger resources. Selecting a program in a large city means that the total resources, both social and business, of that city will be at your disposal. Who would question the potential advantages of New York for its access to the financial centers of the world, or the international communities of San Francisco and Los Angeles for their access to the Pacific Rim economies? With the opportunities and the temptations these cities offer, however, exists the possibility that they will distract you from your MBA experience.

What are the characteristics of programs located in the major cities? First and foremost these programs offer opportunities for higher paying part-time professional work experience, for establishing business-community connections, and for opportunities to work on projects in arrangement with the local MBA programs. If you are married and your spouse is going to work full-time to contribute to your living costs, then the number of employment opportunities will most certainly be greater in a large city, an attribute that may be a major consideration. Access by the faculty to these same opportunities also provides them with opportunities for consulting and research, which can then be brought into the classroom to enhance the quality of your experience. Classroom, club, or other group presentations by executives at all levels and from numerous industries are frequent on-campus occurrences in large cities. Finally, the well-developed transportation facilities of large cities give recruiters better access to graduates.

Some of these advantages can also detract from your MBA experience. Perhaps the most tempting are the part-time work opportunities to ease some of the financial burden you are incurring to attend a program. The more time you spend away from campus, the less the likelihood you will establish relationships with your classmates, contacts that may play a much more important role in your future than you can imagine. Another important consideration that detracts from the glamour of some big-city programs is the cost of apartment rental near the university. The costs of rentals in San Francisco, Chicago, Boston, Los Angeles, and New York City are known to be quite high.

In addition, some large-city programs are not located in the safest areas of the city, which may add some apprehension to the treks that students make to and from the university. Finally, those same opportunities that make faculty better resources for you can become so attractive, lucrative, and tempting that they make faculty inaccessible to you beyond classroom time.

If you consider the opposites of the comments made regarding programs located in large cities, you will get a good perspective of the potential advantages and problems of programs in smaller cities. One important point that demands emphasis is that the sum total of your life will likely revolve around the program and its constituents.

International Business

The meteoric rise of interest in international business is understandable given the economic relationships that now exist throughout the world. Recognition of the fact that we are a world of interrelated and interwoven economies has expanded perceptions of business to include global economic perspectives. The interests and the earnings of global companies, opportunities for investment in emerging markets, and changing political configurations around the world have caused many schools to add international components to their programs or to expand the ones they have. Even schools located far from the centers of international activity have added international specializations as options within the curriculum. Required international courses, the offering of an international MBA or an international dual degree, study abroad opportunities, international internships, area studies tracts, extracurricular cultural programs, and projects abroad are some of the features now found in MBA programs.

If you are interested in international business, must you enroll in a program with an international specialization? Not necessarily, but there is some advantage to doing so. There are three separate considerations that you must weigh: selecting a path for entering the international scene; developing an understanding of the culture; and determining the strength of a program's international connections.

There are two ways to enter the international scene. One way is to enroll in a program that features international study as part of its curriculum or in a program that is located in your country or region of preference. Included in this curriculum will be courses devoted to international topics as well as ways to develop language skills and knowledge of cultures of interest. Being able to spend some time in the country of your choice through an internship or program of study will greatly add to your education and to your employability. Implicit in the availability of such internship or study abroad opportunities is that connections have been established—connections that can lead to employment opportunities upon program completion.

A second way to enter the international arena is to select an MBA program according to the interests that are most important to you. Do not focus solely on international considerations but instead on overall program content. While enrolled, take those courses of interest to you. Then, after graduation, seek employment with a firm that has an international base, initially accepting a position in your area of interest and ability. Once you are working for the firm, you can focus on a way to move into the firm's international arena, pursuing openings as they arise.

Regardless of the path you choose, to move into the international arena it is not enough to just be interested or to have taken international courses. In order to greatly enhance your chances of employment, you should have some background in the country of choice. The need for language skills is presumed. You must also have an understanding of the culture. Making the investment required to travel to your country of preference, living in the culture of that country, and preferably working in that culture, even if only for a summer or a semester, will dramatically increase your credibility and substantiate your commitment and interest.

Selecting a school located in or close to a city with a strong international base will also help your cause. New York, San Francisco, and Los Angeles are cities that immediately come to mind. Atlanta, Houston, New Orleans, Miami, and Chicago are other possibilities.

There are also some "inland" universities that have established strong international reputations and connections in the international arena. The University of South Carolina, the American Graduate School of Management (frequently referred to as *Thunderbird*), and the University of Michigan are three that fall into this category. You should also look to the larger universities because many of them have international resources or may be able to quickly add international elements to their programs.

What Is Accreditation?

Accreditation is a process in which the quality of a program is evaluated according to guidelines and standards established by member school representatives. The most widely recognized business degree program accrediting agency is the AACSB—The International Association for Management Education (formerly known as the American Assembly of Collegiate Schools of Business)—which has a membership roster of over 300 member schools. In order to receive the AACSB's stamp of approval, a program must meet the standards established by the agency. Before issuing its stamp, the agency examines a program for the existence of a clear mission statement; a clear focus and worthwhile course content; terminally qualified, full-time faculty; adequate library and other physical facilities; and class characteristics, among other elements. Periodic reviews are made to ensure that the standards established by the agency have been maintained and that attempts have been made to improve the educational process over time.

Accreditation by agencies other than the AACSB reflects some of the same concerns as the AACSB but focuses on other academic issues. Over 400 schools have received accreditation by meeting the standards of one of six other major, regionally based agencies.

Does accreditation guarantee the quality of a program? Absolutely not. It does mean, however, that the program has passed through a screen of guidelines for quality. Does the requirement of a minimal level of qualified faculty ensure that you will have excellent teachers? Absolutely not. The standards establish qualifications for classroom responsibility, not for effectiveness in the classroom. The standards have as their goal the establishment of quality, but they do not guarantee it. Does the lack of AACSB accreditation mean that a program is inferior? Perhaps not, but if you are looking at one that is not accredited, then it behooves you to extensively and thoroughly evaluate its characteristics to ensure that it will meet your needs and add value to your profile in the eyes of future employers.

Beginning the Decision-Making Process

You are about to make a $100,000 to $125,000 investment decision. In order to make a better decision, you will need to make an up-front investment in some information resources. Because each program will have an application fee, if you can reduce the number of programs to which you apply, then you can easily recoup your investment. And, if you make a better decision about the program to attend, your money will have been well spent.

There are over 1,000 MBA programs in the United States. Some of these were started by schools that jumped onto the MBA bandwagon during the late 1970s and the 1980s, either to generate additional revenue or in response to the pressures by some corporate sponsors to offer graduate study to enhance educational access for their employees. If you are currently employed by and totally committed to staying at a company heavily committed to a specific program or if you have a dedicated commitment to a specific, limited geographical area, then these local programs represent a viable option. Additional reasons for considering these programs include having the self-satisfaction of extending your knowledge base, being able to say you have an MBA, or believing that you have no other MBA alternatives given your current circumstances (in which case you might want to reconsider your decision to pursue the MBA at this time). If none of these considerations weigh heavily in your decision, then you owe it to yourself to take a careful look at whether completing a local program will add significant value to your professional credentials.

If you are considering the widest range of programs, then you should start with the AACSB's Web site at http://www.aacsb.edu. You also may want to have at your disposal *The Official Guide to MBA Programs*, which is published jointly by the Educational Testing Service and the Graduate Management Admissions Council, the latter of which can be viewed as a university-based advisory board to the testing and admissions process. Brief, one-page descriptions of approximately 500 domestic and fifty non-U.S. graduate business programs are found in this basic reference. All but a few of the more than 300 AACSB-accredited programs are referenced and identified in this source. Approximately 200 programs accredited by agencies other than the AACSB are also included. You will find the tabular summary of each university's program and student profiles useful in identifying programs of interest to you. You can then reference the university-provided program information segments, which include brief profiles of each school's location and history, brief descriptions of the programs, admission characteristics, expense projections, financial assistance information, brief placement comments, and addresses. With this reference base you can then begin to solicit information. You may, however, want to wait until you go through the next step before you solicit information.

Next, you should seriously consider buying from one to three references that specifically describe ranked programs. Each of these will probably contain in-depth recommendations which you should employ in your selection process. Such references will vary from reviewing only the "top ten" schools to more than fifty. Non-U.S. programs may or may not be included in these references.

A limited list of references is provided in the appendix for your convenience and to help get you started in this next step in your journey. Two that are recommended because of the number of schools included and the characteristics discussed are *A Business Week Guide—The Best Business Schools* published by McGraw-Hill, and *The Princeton Review: The Best Business Schools.* In addition you should have the latest articles ranking and discussing the top MBA programs, which are published every March by *U.S. News and World Report* and in October of even-numbered years in *Business Week.* You might also check other popular sources such as *Fortune, Time, The Wall Street Journal*, and *Newsweek* in addition to other issues of *Business Week* and *U.S. News and World Report* for recent articles discussing all types of issues relevant to the current status and perceptions of MBA programs. Once you have completed your review of the recommended material you should have narrowed your search to programs of interest to you. Then you can, with the addresses provided in *The Official Guide to MBA Programs* and other sources, either e-mail or write the schools of interest for more detailed information on their programs.

Efficient Ways to Expand Your Program Search

There are several other ways besides writing for information to find out more about programs that interest you. One of the most effective is to attend one of the MBA forums held in major cities throughout the United States, Asia, Europe, and Mexico in the fall and winter months. Not only will these forums enable you to meet with representatives of at least sixty-five programs, you will have the opportunity to attend seminars relevant to the MBA application process. The dates and locations for these forums can be found in the *GMAC Official Guide*, can be obtained by contacting the GMAC, or can be obtained by contacting the MBA office of a local university. Other MBA tours will introduce you to additional programs.

A second alternative is found in career-day programs offered in a great number of cities. These may be more convenient and less costly to attend than MBA forums. Generally speaking, the MBA programs represented at these career days will be more geographically limited than those represented in the MBA forums. Another option is to turn the tables by encouraging programs to come to you. Do this by participating in the Graduate Management Admission Search Service, a part of the GMAT process, in which information you provide plus your exam scores are made available to universities that have subscribed to the service. The universities provide profiles of interest to the service which then matches candidates with those profiles and sends lists of appropriate candidates to each subscribing program. If a university then contacts you on the basis of your profile, you will at least know that there is a possible match of interests.

Changing MBA Program Philosophies

There was a period in the early 1990s during which the luster seemed to have worn off the MBA degree. Some of the reasons given for this decline in popularity were graduates' demand for unjustifiable salaries, their reputation for greed, programs' penchant for developing short-sighted decision makers, graduates' lack of respect for other economic systems and philosophies, their unwillingness to work with others as a team, and their failure to respect the contributions others can make to resolving problems. MBA programs were criticized for their sameness and lack of innovation. Whatever the reasons, schools reevaluated their program content and the perspectives and attitudes being engendered in their graduates. However, the few changes that were made were viewed as superficial and cosmetic, lacking in real substance and failing to represent any change in direction.

In response, program administrators took the criticism to heart and introduced major and substantive changes into their programs and into their educational philosophies. In reaction to the isolationist criticism, for example, options were added to better reflect the international arena. Courses on ethics sprouted up like spring wheat on the plains in reaction to criticisms that greed dominated the value systems of MBAs. Group projects became fashionable and are now generally the norm. Many of the recommended changes have now been made and degree requirements and program philosophies have, for the most part, stabilized. Despite the changes, however, you should, as part of your investigative process, inquire about any program modifications being considered.

The Structure and Culture of MBA Programs

It is important to consider the issue of culture that characterizes each MBA program. This culture will have an immeasurable impact upon your experience with the program. If you select a program with a culture that does not match your personality and objectives, the likelihood of your having a less than positive experience increases dramatically. You might spend thousands upon thousands of dollars and thousands of hours of hard, demanding effort only to end up with a negative experience and attitude. It is your responsibility to discern the cultural characteristics of the programs you are considering to ensure that there is a fit between the program you choose and your needs.

The ways programs accomplish their educational objectives within broad-based frameworks are as varied as the number of programs. Still, the relative approaches can be reduced to four basic instructional approaches: lecture, case study, group projects, and simulation (the representation of business activities and problems via computer models). Nearly all programs will use some combination of these methods, but not all methods will be given equal utilization in all programs. Some programs will place heavy reliance on the use of computers to simulate the business environment. Harvard and the Darden School (Virginia) are renowned for their exclusive reliance on the case method. Harvard has, however, recently become more receptive to marginally moving away from this singularly focused orientation. The exclusive reliance on the case method also appears to be under some limited degree of reconsideration at Darden. The antithesis of the case approach is found in the highly quantitative, conceptual approach of the University of Chicago.

Just as every program differs in its combined use of these four approaches, every instructor will teach his or her classes in a slightly different manner. However, all business schools tend to build their faculties over time to reflect the school's underlying philosophy of business education. In most cases, this means you can expect to find and use a mixture of quantitative, qualitative, case, problematic, conceptual, and applied approaches in your course work.

Each program will also tend to admit students who reflect its educational philosophy. In what type of educational environment will you thrive? Do you prefer to delve into theoretical concepts or to focus on practical solutions? Are you more interested in the thought process and conceptual underpinnings of a topic or whether the concept can be immediately applied? Do you relish the challenge of thinking through complex mathematical formulas to generate a precise number? Do you anticipate spending hour after hour in front of a computer screen attacking the situation that has been presented to you? Do you prefer a psychologically supportive setting in which you are able to become familiar with approaches and concepts and to learn the relevant questions to ask? A portion of the application process is designed to discern how you will react to these varying educational philosophies.

The degree of intraclass competition generally sets the tone of the culture. Some schools foster the position that it is every person for himself or herself. So, if you thrive on hard-nosed, one-on-one competition, then this type of program is for you. A case-based program in a highly competitive environment will demand classroom interaction and participation. Are you the type who will speak up and jump into the fray to defend your position against others? Do you have the type of personality that will thrive on the competition? Are you the type of person who feels comfortable in an environment that swirls around you and you alone because it matches your abilities and talents against all others?

Or do you prefer the dynamics of a group and the thrill of getting the job done in a group context? Your response to this question is becoming increasingly important given the recent changes in emphasis on group versus individual performance. The group emphasis was added as a result of criticism by the business world that little to nothing is accomplished by an individual working in isolation. Instead, most real-world work is accomplished by individuals working in a team context. The employment market spoke; there was little choice but to listen. Many programs have made this adjustment; others have not, will not, or are in the process of adapting.

Most of the references suggested earlier have sections on the culture of each program. You need to determine whether a program is competitive or cooperative, intense or relaxed, and social or individualistic. Other characteristics you will want to evaluate are the average age of entering students, the dispersion of undergraduate degrees earned, the percentage of students having work experience, and the average number of years and types of work experience students have. Additional factors such as the undergraduate grade-point averages, GMAT scores, and percentage of students entering directly from undergraduate programs will provide additional insight into the makeup of the class culture.

Once you have developed your select list of programs, a campus visit will help you evaluate the culture in person. No matter what method you use to evaluate a program's culture, respect the fact that the culture will be a very important factor in the quality of your MBA experience and in your perception of the true value of your multi-thousand dollar investment.

Reputation Versus Accessibility of Faculty

Each university will make the maximum possible effort to impress you with the credentials of its faculty. However, just because these high achievers are on the faculty does not mean that you will derive any benefit from them. One reason is that they may be so involved in their own personal success that their instructional role may be quite minor. That is, they may meet their classes at the appointed time, share their knowledge with you at that time, and otherwise make themselves unavailable beyond their minimum commitments, opting instead to use their time for research or consulting purposes. Another reason relates to executive education. Many schools have found executive education to be a lucrative reputation builder and opt to assign their prestigious faculty to teach in executive MBA and executive education programs. Thus, well-known professors may not even have classroom responsibilities in the programs you are considering, even though program literature will not publicize this fact.

Teaching Effectiveness

Access and reputation are one thing: teaching ability is another. As you conduct your investigation of programs, one conclusion you will reach is that program reputation and faculty names in no way guarantee effectiveness in the classroom. Every program will have its excellent and its ineffective teachers. To their credit, many schools have programs in place for students to evaluate the quality of the teaching in the classes they take. These evaluations are then made available to students considering taking the class in the future and may be made available to prospective students while visiting campus (it is much more difficult to obtain copies of these evaluations by mail). Some programs have worked to enhance teaching effectiveness in response to continual, pervasive criticisms. However, even schools that have improved their teaching may still be more concerned with their research than with their teaching reputation.

Once you have developed your list of top choices, partly based on what you have read about the schools' quality of teaching, you should visit campuses of choice so that you can assess the teaching effectiveness and class culture for yourself. Most schools will not only introduce you to their current students so that you may elicit their perceptions of teaching effectiveness, but they also will strongly encourage you to visit classes.

Placement Facilities

The nature of the placement process for an MBA is changing and you had best be prepared for it. The days of Fortune 500 companies serving as perpetual fountains of employment appear to be over. Medium-sized and smaller, newer firms appear to be the areas of greater opportunity. Placement offices across the country are in the process of adjusting to this new environment.

Do not start out with the presumption that interviews will be readily accessible to you. Some placement offices have found it necessary to control the interviewing process by implementing bidding systems or other measures to allocate the limited number of interview slots available in a company's interview schedule. It is your responsibility to investigate and to evaluate the placement facilities and policies as part of your program selection process. It is your responsibility to know what the process is for getting on an interview schedule and to know what that process implies for the probability of having access to companies that are important to you. The bottom line is that you need to do more for yourself in the placement arena than rely upon the school's placement office to do everything for you.

Not only must your perspective of the placement function change, but also the questions you ask when evaluating programs. It is still pertinent to ask what companies interview on campus, but do not stop there. Inquire about the number of graduates recently placed with those firms and the projected rate of placement. Also inquire about initiatives being taken in light of the changing placement market. How developed are the placement support activities? Are there workshops on every aspect of the placement process? Are specialists available to help you develop and revise your resume? Are facilities available to videotape and critique mock interviews in order to maximize your interviewing skills? Are specialized workshops or other sources built into the system to help you improve your verbal and written communication skills? Has the number of persons devoted to the placement function changed? Are there any expansion plans? Are there alumni working for particular companies of interest to you whom you can contact about the strength of the program's reputation and who will enhance your chances of being placed with that firm? Are mentor relationships in place that will help you establish contacts within that company?

If there is no direct pipeline to the companies of interest to you, do you have sufficient belief in both yourself and the record you intend to establish in the program that you can develop your own network? If your answer is yes, then perhaps some of these questions will not be that important for you.

Location, Program Size, and the Placement Effort

The relationship between program size and placement success warrants special attention because of its importance to your placement considerations. Normally, the larger the graduating class, the easier is the placement effort. This is obvious: The larger the number of graduates, the greater the number of candidates who can be interviewed and the greater the opportunity for a firm to find that individual with the characteristics it seeks. Thus, the likelihood of having a successful recruiting trip offsets any inconveniences of getting to a campus located in an out-of-the-way city. Small programs located in smaller and less accessible cities will encounter greater challenges in their placement efforts, particularly if the programs do not have some offsetting strengths. Offsetting strengths can come from a selective admissions process; a reasonable graduating class size; unique program qualities; an established and known expertise in one or more functional areas, preferably combined with strong faculty identification and contacts; and/or a highly effective, dedicated placement staff, preferably connected to an effective alumni network.

The relationship between program location and placement success is also important to consider. Even the very best programs with nationwide visibility tend to have regional identities in terms of their placement patterns. The West Coast programs have their pipelines to Silicon Valley, Los Angeles, and San Francisco. New York, Washington D.C., and Route 128 outside of Boston have their identification with the major East Coast programs. Northwestern and the University of Chicago have their strongest connections in Chicago and the other major Midwest cities but also stretch to both coasts. Some schools have difficulty attracting corporate recruiters despite the strengths of their programs because of the strong geographical employment biases of their graduates. Graduates of southeastern programs generally avoid the harshness of northern weather. The Dallas–Fort Worth and Houston metroplexes attract many southwestern graduates, as does the West Coast. If you have a regional preference, it is in your best interest to carefully consider strong programs in that region in addition to those that are viewed as having nationwide recognition and respect.

Choosing to attend a program with a strong regional identity will somewhat hinder your degree mobility and may require you to take more time to find your initial position if you are looking in a different geographical area. While you might have to look for two to four weeks in any given city with a degree from the top schools, it may take you six weeks to three months to land that same position with a strong regional degree and strong placement profile. Still, landing the position is not impossible; it's just a bigger challenge. Once you get a position, your success will depend upon your ability and other factors. Also be cognizant of the fact that your choosing a city outside the area will also mean that the alumni network will not be as strong as it would for graduates from programs in that area.

Mentor Programs

A relatively new feature of many MBA programs is *mentoring*, in which a member of the business community agrees to take a limited number of students under his or her tutelage as a way of further introducing them to the real-world aspects of the business environment. Ideally, a mentor is employed in your field of interest, and program administrators do all they can to ensure this is the case.

The quality and the value of any mentoring relationship will vary with the mentor. Work demands, personal demands, and personal commitment will all play a role. An excellent mentor will introduce you to your field of interest, provide you with direction for success within that field, and help you develop contacts. Issues that you should investigate before selecting a program, then, include whether a mentoring program is in place, the stage of development of the program, the fields that have mentoring relationships in place, and, if your area of interest is not included, the potential for establishing mentoring in that area.

Mentoring can provide an invaluable opportunity. If a school does not have mentoring in place, then take the initiative to establish such a relationship for yourself. Make every effort to make it work.

Program Identities

Each program will have its own program identity. Programs might be strong in developing skills and abilities conducive to consulting, to the heady world of investments, to marketing management, to manufacturing, to technology management, to international business, or to commercial banking and so on. It is your responsibility to determine these areas of identity and to assess them in terms of their value to you.

You may lack sufficient business experience to know whether an area is of interest to you. However, the first year of your MBA will be a wide-ranging experience so that when the time comes for you to make a decision about your area of specialization, you will be able to do so. The only way to resolve this contradiction is to pick that program which appears to best meet your other criteria, being comfortably assured that placement efforts will be exerted on your behalf regardless of your field of concentration or specialization.

Part-Time Considerations

On average, a two-year program on a part-time basis will take a minimum of three years to complete. The normal course load when working full-time is two courses per semester and one course during the summer. Five courses per year in a twenty-course program results in a minimum four-year commitment, assuming that you keep on schedule and encounter no diversions.

That is four years of constant pressure to balance the demands of your professional career, your personal and family life, and your academic life. About halfway through, the excitement will wane and you will proceed on sheer determination and commitment. You will go home tired and still have your next obligation to meet, whether it be something for your job, your classes, or your personal situation. Your Saturdays and Sundays will still involve errands and social commitments plus academic demands and any work you have brought home from the office.

Some universities are now reviewing their part-time programs with the intent of reducing this lengthy time period. A commitment of between two and three years seems to be the revised objective for program length.

Three other considerations add gloom to the part-time experience. Perhaps the most discouraging is the strong tendency for companies to ignore your completion of the MBA despite the money they have invested in you and despite the effort you have expended. That is, your employer will congratulate you for having completed the program and then it will likely be business as usual with respect to your assignments. While you were in school, your company may have spent time and money to recruit recent full-time graduates into positions for which you are now qualified and that you would like to have. You may find yourself having to or at least wanting to change jobs.

The second consideration relates to perceptions of the worth of an MBA earned in a part-time program versus that earned in a full-time capacity. Traditionally, the full-time experience has been more highly valued, particularly in the short-term. That is, the presumption is that a student who attends full-time is able to completely focus upon the academic experience and accordingly gains the maximum benefit possible from that experience. In contrast, a student who attends part-time is perceived to have a somewhat dissipated experience, having to spread energies over a range of activities. After a period of time, however, your ability and your having earned the MBA will be the important consideration; the fact that you earned it on a part-time basis will no longer be an issue.

There is one last consideration in part-time study that demands mention because if it occurs, it is highly frustrating. Recall that a reasonable estimate for completion of a part-time program is currently three to four years. If you are the competent, high achiever presumed to be reading this book, your chances of receiving a major promotion within that time period are quite good. What if that promotion requires a transfer out of the region? Unlike undergraduate hours, graduate hours are generally not transferable or are transferable to only a very limited extent. A further complication is the fact that part-time programs have a limited time period for completion, for example six or seven years with provisions for (but no guarantees of approvals for) extensions of one or two years. The chance of your being transferred back within these time constraints is relatively low. Would you be willing to travel extensively to complete the program if you were near its end at the time of your transfer? Would you be willing to start over again in your new location? Or would you just give up?

4

Understanding the Admissions Process

In this chapter, you will be introduced to the inner workings of the admissions process, primarily from the perspective of the admissions committee. The focus of this chapter is to help you better understand that process and the interactions of the people within that process. The objective is to make the decision process less intimidating to you. It is important for you to recognize that it is the intent of the committees of the vast majority of MBA programs to admit students, not to reject them. Therefore, you should view yourself as someone the committee will want to admit and approach the process accordingly.

The process is designed to give you every consideration. You, in turn, must give that process the utmost respect. Specifically, you should plan to devote at least sixty to eighty hours to completing your applications, assuming that you are going to be applying to at least four or five programs.

What Is the Admissions Committee?

When your file is complete with essays, transcripts, GMAT scores, and letters of recommendation, it is ready to be evaluated by the admissions committee. The forms such committees take are as varied as the programs to which you submit applications, but each will have the objective of admitting students and each will examine the same basic issues. The objective to admit assures you that your file will be thoroughly read and professionally evaluated.

The one commonality across programs is that there will be an administrator in charge of the process. In most cases, this person will play a far greater role than simply ensuring that your folder is complete and that it gets properly handled in the review process. At smaller schools, the director and his or her staff or assistants may be the committee. Some schools have committees with two or three people, and some with as many as ten. An advisory committee may provide guidance about the policies to be implemented, such as class size, class diversity (liberal arts versus engineering versus business majors, for example), and work experience. Or this second-level committee may consist of the people who will actually review the applications and make the admit decision. Usually, this committee will consist of faculty members, but some schools have added students, alumni, and even psychologists. In some schools, the admissions staff is empowered to make decisions based upon stated and approved criteria (a combination of grade-point average, GMAT score, and years of work experience, for example). In some programs, particularly the larger ones, directors may not see all or even a majority of files.

Regardless of the structure, throughout the process the director will play a significant role. Frequently, the director will be asked to give an opinion on those applicants about whom the committee cannot decide. Or the director can take the initiative to present a file that has caught his or her attention. The director, in conjunction with the admissions staff, may be given the responsibility to segregate the applicant pool into three categories—those who are "clear admits" using the school's criteria, those who do not currently meet the acceptance criteria, and those who are "borderline." At many schools, all decisions concerning applicants are actually made by the entire committee, but even in this case the director plays a role in presenting your file to the committee and in discussing your file. Recognize and respect the fact that the director plays a continuous, influential role throughout the process.

Regardless of either the structure or the process, note that someone of influence will thoroughly read your file. Your first objective is to be classified as someone the program wants, regardless of the qualifications of any other applicants. Should you not fall into that category, then your objective is to make the borderline category (every school has one) and to then so impress the reviewers that you are selected. You do this by conveying that you possess an unusual background, are interesting and unique, will contribute to the program, are properly prepared to enter the program (particularly in terms of your quantitative skills), will complete the program, and will represent the program in an impressive way after completion.

Who Is on the Committee?

The individuals on the admissions committee will represent a wide range of personalities, interests, and experiences. The elements they have in common are a dedication to admitting the best possible applicants to the program; an ability to read analytically, to listen closely to the opinion of others, and to clearly and forcefully express their opinions; an ability to accurately evaluate potential and "fit" in terms of the culture of the program; and a willingness to make decisions in this context. Each member will offer input and exert influence upon the decision, reflecting his or her distinct personality and perspective.

Generally, representatives of the various academic departments are committee members. This suggests that if you have expressed an intent to focus your elective course work in a particular area, then the representative from that area may exert greater influence in the final decision.

Most committee members will have been a part of the school in one capacity or another for some time. Seldom are new faculty members appointed to the committee because it is in their best interest to devote their time to those accomplishments that will get them promotion and/or tenure. This means that committee members are usually familiar with the program and its culture. They are in a position to determine whether you will be a positive addition to the classroom and the overall culture of the school and will evaluate your file in this context.

To better understand the process, recognize that admissions staff face many pressure-packed issues. They have the responsibility of implementing and administering the school's overall admissions policy, whereas the individual decisions may be left to the judgment of others who comprise a committee designated for such purposes. The school's dean often articulates the overall mission in the school's literature so prospective MBAs can better understand what type of students might benefit from the program. There is a great interest in enrolling a diverse class in terms of life experience, work experience, ethnicity, gender, cultural background, geographical representation, and personality. You will rarely find these policies quantified, but admissions directors know what groups and interests must be represented and are well aware of their responsibilities to represent them.

Now that you are aware of these issues, it is up to you to take advantage of them at every opportunity. Carefully, systematically, and objectively review your profile in light of each of these considerations. Focus on your unique and interesting qualities.

An Overview of the Admissions Process

The admissions committee must make tough choices from among many equally qualified and capable candidates. Applicants are presented, recommendations are made by the reviewers, discussion and debate are undertaken, and a decision is reached. The committee does its best to admit prospective students on the basis of what sets them apart and in terms of their fit with the culture of the program. A judgment is also made about applicants' ability to meet the academic demands of the course work. Committee members spend long hours of hard work on this difficult process. Once you make it to the committee stage, the decision-making process becomes highly subjective.

Application Strategies

Business schools deny admission to students who are as well qualified as others they admit. The decision to accept or deny is based on the personal and quite subjective views of the people who evaluate your application. While it is impossible to predict who will read your application, there are strategies for battling and offsetting the subjective nature of the process.

At this point in your life, you have probably been through a similar process, perhaps without realizing it, in vying for a job, promotion, or officer's position. Although others were vying for that same position, it was awarded to you. What was it about you that caused you to be selected over your competition? You have to bring that same fervor, commitment, preparedness, persuasion, and excitement to the process of applying to an MBA program. In this case, more than one position is open—but don't slack off, because there are many candidates seeking those slots. You have sold yourself before; it is now time to do it again.

There are at least two people whose attention you want to attract. The first is the one who will initially read your file, usually a member of the admissions staff. Commit to completing your application in such a way that this person becomes so impressed with you that he or she will bring your file to the attention of the committee or the next reader in the process. Catch the attention of these individuals and you are starting to tip the odds of acceptance in your favor.

The second person whose attention you need to attract is often overlooked. If you have an interest in a particular area of study, then you should consider letting the chairperson or department head know about your interest. Send that person a cover letter indicating your interest. Include a professionally prepared resume. Do not—*do not*—replicate your application file. Further, do not expect this person to get directly involved in making a decision about your application unless he or she happens to be a participant in the admissions process. If you have impressed this person, however, there is a high probability that he or she will make some inquiries about your status. Any such show of interest will certainly generate a stronger review of your candidacy.

How Your Case Will Be Decided

Changing applicant pools, criticisms of the programs by corporate America, changing employment opportunities, and efforts to achieve greater diversity in classes have made the selection process seem more mysterious than ever to prospective MBAs. To add to this mystery, the selection process is now more subjective than ever before.

What happens between the time you submit your application and the day you receive that most important letter in the mail? What factors make the difference in the decision?

Regardless of the institution or the makeup of the committee, the decision will be based on the answer to three central questions, ones to which you have already been introduced:

- Does the applicant have the ability to do well in and to complete the program?

- Will the applicant contribute to the program?

- Will the applicant reflect positively upon the program after graduation?

The intent at this point is to focus upon the psychology of the decision-making process. (In the next chapter, we will consider the specifics such as grades, quantitative ability, and work experience.) It is not the questions but the desired responses that have changed over the years.

Regardless of the size of the committee or its specific format, it will use two basic approaches to deciding your case. The first is a "blind read" in which two to three committee members evaluate your application. Each member is purposefully kept unaware of the evaluations of the others. If all agree, then the decision has been made. If only two readers do the blind read and they disagree, then a third opinion is sought in an attempt to resolve the matter. Although one would instinctively presume that with three reviewers there would be no ambiguous outcome, one might be in favor of admitting, one against admitting, and one neutral, not having been impressed one way or the other. A discussion among the three may ensue, or the application may be referred to another element of the committee that will also begin with a blind read, or the file may be forwarded to the head of a department in which the applicant has indicated an intent to study. For this final option to happen, the applicant would have to have exhibited either a very high potential in that particular field of study or have expressed an interest in studying in an area in which the school had particular interest in increasing enrollment. While department heads are involved only infrequently in the application review process, the fact that they are used stresses that the emphasis is on acceptance rather than rejection and that a large element of subjectivity exists throughout the process.

The second approach used by a review committee is to involve each committee member in reading and evaluating each file. This approach, because of the large number of applications that may be involved, is frequently modified for expediency—the committee is broken up into subcommittees with the applications being distributed equally. An alternative process is for the entire committee to review only the file comments. After discussion within each subcommittee, only the most controversial files are presented to the committee as a whole. Again, the important point to note is that your file will be given full and fair consideration.

Chapter 6 will show that objective measures are considered, but in the final analysis the decision is subjectively reached. This is why you may be accepted to some programs and not others. In different programs, different people base their decisions on different objectives that have developed from different foci, cultures, educational philosophies, educational approaches, and so on. Regardless, you must approach the process as though you should and will be accepted by all!

Before we examine the objective criteria, however, we will first consider the issues international students face when applying to and participating in MBA programs. Even if you are not an international student, by familiarizing yourself with their particular concerns you will develop a better understanding of the role you will play in a program and enhance your relationships and interactions with your fellow international students.

5

Focus on
International
Applicants*

This chapter deals with topics that are of particular interest to international applicants to U.S. business schools. Other chapters in this book detail the techniques for presenting yourself effectively to the schools you have selected. Here, the focus is on four major topics: gaining admission, acquiring good skills in English, preparing to enter an MBA program, and acclimating to life in the United States. To gain the most from this book, we suggest that you read the succeeding chapters after completing this one.

Are U.S. Business Schools Interested in Accepting International Students?

There should be no doubt in any applicant's mind about the interest of U.S. business schools in international students. Every business school wants to enroll the best possible students, a fact continuously stressed throughout this book. Since business increasingly occurs on a global level, the perspectives and insights of international students

*By Nancy Roth Remington, Director of International Programs, Goizueta Business School, Emory University

are an integral part of the learning environment that business schools seek to foster. Many schools actively recruit international students in an effort to create an MBA student body representative of the marketplace. Most programs recruit students with a variety of functional business experiences, undergraduate majors, and extracurricular interests, as well as national and ethnic backgrounds. The reason for assembling such a varied group is not merely to enhance the statistical profile of each entering class of students; it is to create a strong learning environment featuring active, searching dialogue among a diverse and vibrant community of students and faculty.

Since the early 1990s, an increasing number of business schools have worked to expand the size of the international populations in their MBA degree programs. It is now common for international students to represent 20 to 25 percent of the student population in many highly regarded programs, with this percentage sometimes rising to as much as 50 percent. For international applicants, this interest on the part of business schools offers an opportunity and a challenge. Your success in convincing the school of your choice to select you rests on your ability to make a compelling argument about how you will contribute to the program. You must be able to articulate your goals and qualifications coherently within the context of the specific attributes desired by each of the MBA programs to which you are applying.

Customizing your applications means that you will first need to take the time to research a variety of MBA programs. Then you must demonstrate throughout your application that you have the English fluency and quantitative preparation needed for study in the MBA program. Your research may lead you to consider programs that were previously unknown to you, for the United States offers an enormous number of options for MBA education. There are about 800 business schools, just over 300 of which are accredited by the AACSB (International Association for Management Education), the largest accrediting body for management education. As indicated in other chapters in this book, schools have many different attributes; therefore, it is wise to carefully review characteristics of these programs—such as size of student body, school location, special programs, international activities—and not only rank when determining which schools you will target.

Many schools offer multiple formats for granting the MBA degree—the traditional two-year daytime programs, one-year and one-year accelerated programs, multiyear evening programs for young working professionals, and executive MBA programs for managers with extensive work experience. The appendix lists a number of books that contain profiles of MBA programs available throughout the United States.

Visas and Visa Status

From the perspective of U.S. business schools, who are international students? Some schools count every student who does not hold a U.S. passport, including permanent residents who carry "green cards." Other programs do not include permanent residents, whose legal status permits them to receive financial compensation for their work in the United States without obtaining special permission or following specific guidelines. Most international students hold either J-1 or F-1 visas, which grant them the legal right to remain in the United States for a specific amount of time in order to study. Normally, a student visa begins two to four weeks before the start of an educational program and ends shortly after the student graduates or completes his or her course of study. Visa status is usually not a consideration when admissions officers are reviewing an applicant's file. However, it can be an important factor in the awarding of scholarships and loans, because some MBA programs do not award tuition scholarships to international students, and most loan programs require the signature of a U.S. citizen.

What Are U.S. Business Schools Looking For?

Admissions committees recognize that the decision to enter a graduate management program requires a tremendous commitment of time, energy, and in most cases, financial resources. For international students, the commitment is even greater. Patrick Noonan, MBA program director at the Goizueta Business School of Emory University explains it this way:

> All MBA students must simultaneously grapple with many challenging transitions when they decide to attend a graduate management pro-

gram. Some of the most frequent include going into debt and losing their salaries, since the vast majority of MBA students have at least two years of work experience; understanding MBA performance standards and the norms of MBA culture, which are different from those in many other undergraduate programs; spending a great deal of their time working in teams and receiving "team" grades regardless of individual contribution to a given project; and moving to the location of their MBA program.

International students face all of these adjustments as well as many other significant challenges: living away from family and friends in an unfamiliar country; understanding different social/cultural behaviors and expectations; eating unfamiliar food, trying to locate the ingredients for "home cooking," and in some cases, learning to cook; learning when and how to ask for help; and studying in a second language at the graduate level. International students must also adjust to the "student-centered," interactive approach to learning that underlies the academic environment in U.S. business school programs, an approach that requires students to be full partners in the learning process and proactive producers of knowledge.

Admission officers and faculty members understand this phenomenon and appreciate the energy and commitment of international students. Most readily recognize that they themselves could not venture to a non-English-speaking country to attend graduate school because they lack the required linguistic skill; therefore, U.S. staff and professors regard the applications of international students with respect and admiration. This does not mean, however, that admissions officers set aside admissions standards when evaluating applications from international candidates. It is up to each applicant to demonstrate their academic preparation and English language skills and to reveal the value he or she will bring to classroom discussion and the school's MBA community.

Creating an Effective Application

This book devotes many chapters to an in-depth analysis of each part of the MBA application. What follows are some insights that should be particularly useful for international applicants in approaching the complex process of applying to business schools in the United States. As you read this section, remember that admissions committees consider all parts of an application to be important, although schools may choose to give different weights to different parts. Committees evaluate everything in a candidate's file—which will include the completed application as well as correspondence, e-mails, and interview notes—in an effort to determine whether the applicant is a good match for their particular program.

To create an effective application, you must first define your career and educational goals. After you select the schools of greatest interest, you will need to devote time to understanding their specific attributes so that you can "speak" to the interests of these schools throughout your application. You can accomplish this in many ways: by reading these schools' literature, visiting Web sites, asking questions of friends and colleagues who have attended (or know someone who has attended) these schools, and by referencing the sources listed in the appendix.

Elements of the Application

Academic Background

The first issue for admissions committees is to determine if you can successfully handle the academic program. Grades from each university attended are reviewed carefully, because your academic record along with the quality of your previous educational institution are often the best predictors of success in an MBA program. The admissions committee will look at the courses you have taken, your performance, and your rank in your class (if available).

If grading in your particular school, or in your country, is known to be particularly hard, you may want to note this on your application so that your accomplishments can be evaluated fairly. For example, in Indonesia, a grade-point average (GPA) of 3.1 (on a 4.0 scale) might place students in the top 2 to 3 percent of their class. Conversely, in many of the countries of the former Soviet Union, there is severe grade inflation. In either case, your class rank will be very important. It is more persuasive for an explanation of grading to come from the institution itself or an independent advising office, such as the Fulbright

Commission. It is also very helpful to include a grading evaluation sheet in your application.

If your university transcript shows any weaknesses, either in subject areas or during specific time periods, be prepared to explain why. Illness, family crisis, financial difficulties in a family business, or political instability in your country might help to explain poor grades at a particular time. (You may need to document these claims in order for them to be given serious consideration.) While these issues are highly sensitive and you may feel awkward mentioning them to strangers, you will find that admissions officers will greatly appreciate your honesty and your ability to straightforwardly address problems you have faced.

Admissions committees are particularly interested in seeing what, if any, quantitatively oriented courses you have taken because, in most instances, MBA studies will require a good familiarity with algebra and statistical concepts. This mathematical background is especially important in classes such as economics, finance, and business statistics that are required core courses in most MBA programs. If a school you are targeting has a preadmission requirement you have not covered in your university curriculum (such as calculus or statistics), make sure to communicate where and how you plan to fulfill the requirement.

GMAT and TOEFL Exams

Standardized tests are not a perfect measure of an applicant's abilities; however, they do give admissions committees an objective means for comparing MBA applicants from a variety of academic backgrounds. Schools set their own standards for using these test scores, and all schools consider standardized test scores as one element in the MBA application. In succeeding chapters, you will find a great deal written about how to prepare for the GMAT.

Preparing for and taking these tests often causes great anxiety. The first important point to be made is that applicants should not take these tests without committed and focused preparation. Before sitting for the exam, make sure you are familiar with the test format and instructions so you do not waste precious time. The second point is that continuous test taking—namely, taking the tests more than three times—is seldom effective in significantly raising scores in weak areas. Because the GMAT is now administered on computer, candidates should practice typing in English as part of their preparation; a lack of proficiency in typing has resulted in lower scores on the AWA (Analytical Writing Assessment) section for some applicants. Older GMAT test takers should refamiliarize themselves with high school math since this, too, is an important part of the quantitative portion of the test.

TOEFL and GMAT scores are analyzed in several ways. Admissions committees review not only the total score, but also scores on individual sections of the test. With the GMAT in particular, some schools may establish informal standards for each separate section: verbal, quantitative, and AWA. To gain a more complete sense of an applicant's ability in English, the admissions committee will compare scores on the verbal and writing sections of the GMAT with TOEFL results and university grades in English (where available). To assess writing skills, the committee will then evaluate the essays on the AWA portion of the GMAT along with the essays included in the application. While all schools realize that essays written under time pressure cannot be as polished or elegant as those written under less stressful circumstances, a highly professional application essay that sounds like it has been written by someone other than the applicant may hurt the applicant's chances for admission.

Candidates need to recognize that the TOEFL is only one tool used by schools to evaluate English skills; if the real ability to use English is questionable, as demonstrated in an interview or through poorly written correspondence, the school may not regard the TOEFL as the primary indicator of English ability. Conversely, if a school's minimum TOEFL is 600, it may nonetheless choose to accept an outstanding candidate with only a 590 score if the candidate demonstrates the ability to converse easily and persuasively during an interview and in subsequent e-mail or phone conversations.

A suggestion regarding taking either the TOEFL or the GMAT more than two times: If you are not satisfied with either your English or quantitative scores, wait at least several months before taking the tests again so that you can further prepare for the parts of the test that were difficult for you. Taking the GMAT once each month may raise your overall score by a few points, largely by increasing the score in the area in which you are already most competent; however, this tactic seldom results in any significant improvement on those parts of the test you need to strengthen.

When analyzed together, your grades and standardized test scores enable the admissions committee to make fairly accurate predictions regarding your future academic performance. If the admissions readers are satisfied with this aspect of your application, the committee will then attempt to determine your ability to make a strong contribution to the prospective MBA class and to your profession throughout the course of your career.

Work Experience

Most competitive business schools admit a class in which the average work experience for students is three to six years, and most schools take into account the applicants' levels of responsibility in their jobs. A majority of admitted MBA candidates have two or more years of postuniversity work experience. The exceptions to this policy might include those with responsible work in various capacities in family-owned businesses or significant and continuing employment with major companies or government agencies after several years of part-time work during university studies. If you have fewer than two or three years of full-time, postuniversity work experience, you should include all noteworthy internships on the resume you submit with your application.

In reviewing your resume and evaluating your full-time and/or part-time work experience and internships, admissions committees want to have a full picture of your specific responsibilities and accomplishments. By understanding your experiences at work, they try to project the kinds of contributions you might make to classroom discussions and the ease, or difficulty, with which you might achieve your career goals.

Leadership Skills

Most admissions committees look for candidates who will (1) add value to the school's MBA learning environment by sharing their experiences and knowledge; (2) participate actively in the life of the school, enlivening the MBA community and helping the institution achieve its stated goals; (3) become business managers and leaders in whom the school can take pride; and (4) become alumni who will continue to play active roles in the life of the school after graduation. Assessing your capacity for leadership is, therefore, a very important element in assessing your application and "fit" with the school.

In order to evaluate your potential for leadership, admissions officers will review all activities listed in your application, noting the level of leadership you attained and the breadth and variety of organizations in which you participated. Many essay questions will give you an opportunity to explain your abilities in working with groups and your leadership qualities. Make sure to mention your activities in your undergraduate institution as well as in the community and at your job, indicating if you initiated a particular program and what leadership roles you played. It is also useful to indicate whether you were appointed or elected to these positions.

Recommendation Letters

Evidence of leadership skills can be found not only in a candidate's resume and essays, but also in the confidential letters of recommendation. Therefore, select carefully the individuals who will write your recommendations, including people who know you well enough to discuss specific accomplishments in university, professional, or community activities. If you are a candidate with fewer than three years of work experience, it will be especially valuable for your recommendation letters to note how and under what circumstances you have exercised leadership, and how well you have worked with colleagues who are older than you.

If the people writing your recommendations cannot write in English, it is best if they write their recommendation letters in their native language and provide certified translations; in this way, the admissions committee will have more faith that the letters were, in fact, written by the recommenders and not by you or a professional writer. Recommendation letters should be on letterhead. If letters are printed on plain paper, you should offer an explanation for why letterhead was not used.

Essays

Essays and interviews offer applicants an opportunity to help the admissions committee learn more about their motivations and goals, interests, successes, and challenges they have faced. Most importantly, the readers of your essays want to know how you reflect on what you have done, how you connect your own experiences with bigger issues—in your previous work experience or your life. In effect, the essay gives you a chance to "tell your story."

When possible, in both essays and interviews, use concrete examples. Avoid giving purely philosophical or theoretical answers to questions and remember that in the active learning environment of MBA programs, faculty (and by extension admissions readers) want to know your opinions. Also, do not be afraid to talk about difficulties or failures you have faced if you can describe what you learned as the result of facing such challenges. To make an effective presentation, you should always be ready to discuss situations in which you have shown initiative and, thus, added value to your organization or team. In this way, you will also help admissions committees to view you as a potentially active participant in their programs.

Consider taking advantage of the optional essay topic offered in most applications—"Is there anything else you would like to tell us about yourself?" This question provides you with an opportunity to comment on particular aspects of your life or work and to further convince the admissions committee of the value you can bring to the MBA program. All too often, applicants leave this page blank. If any part of your statistical profile is significantly lower than, or different from, the profile of a school's accepted class, give a straightforward explanation. If you have strengths or serious interests outside your job or academic area of expertise (for example, in athletics, music, chess, or drama), use the optional essay to describe the reasons for your commitment and your accomplishments. This is also an opportunity to discuss unique experiences specific to your culture, country, family, or ethnic background.

Another important issue to address is why you have chosen to apply to a particular school. All admissions readers want to know why you have selected their school, and you can only make a compelling case for yourself if you can discuss the school's specific attributes in terms of your own short- and long-term goals and ambitions. If the school does not provide a specific essay question on this issue, you may use the optional essay already noted.

Interviews

Along with the essays, an interview gives the admissions committee an opportunity to understand more about your background while giving you a chance to learn more about the school (however, not all schools offer interviews). The interviewer's primary goals are to evaluate your comfort with and fluency in English and to assess how you might contribute to MBA class discussions and the MBA community as a whole.

If you can afford the time and money, visit the schools to which you wish to apply. In addition to arranging an interview, try to visit a class and talk with current students. If a campus visit is not possible, contact the school to ask if alumni interviews are possible or if admissions officers will visit your country or region. The Graduate Management Admissions Council Forums and the MBA Tour are only two of the many programs that bring admissions and other business school officers to Asia, Europe, and Latin America during the course of the year. In addition, a number of schools offer telephone interviews. You can expect a campus interview to last from thirty to forty-five minutes and a telephone interview to be a little shorter.

One suggestion regarding essays and interviews: When you are asked to respond to a question, remember to address directly in a clear and concise manner the question that is asked. By including anecdotes and illustrations, you can "bring your answer to life" and help your interviewer understand your work and life experiences. When you provide specific information, try not to get so enmeshed in the details that you lose sight of the answer you wish to give.

Career Goals

Because students and schools attach great importance to post-MBA job placement, admissions committees evaluate applicants' stated career goals in light of job history and previous achievements to determine if their goals are realistic. In a few schools, career services professionals may be asked to read applications and comment on a candidate's likely placement after completing the MBA degree if the admissions committee has concerns about a candidate's career aspirations and post-MBA job placement.

The greatest number of placement concerns arise when a candidate wishes to change career fields (for example, from marketing to finance or manufacturing to general consulting) and at the same time expects to obtain a high-level position with an excellent salary. Placement challenges are compounded when students have relatively little (fewer than two or three years') full-time work experience.

Career services and placement offices offer many programs designed to help enrolled MBA students develop skills that will enable them to take charge of their own job searches. Services vary from school to school. In addition to arranging on-campus interviews with company representatives, most schools will offer workshops in some or all of the following areas: resume writing, interviewing skills, researching companies, creating networks, and international placement. While many students find their internships and jobs through on-campus interviews, networking and effective company research often provide the leads that result in job offers. This means that, in order to conduct a successful job search, you must be proactive, persistent, and creative in making connections.

International students with F-1 and J-1 visas who wish to find internships or jobs in the United States almost always need to spend more time on their job searches than do their U.S. counterparts. This is due to a number of factors: unfamiliarity with U.S. business culture and companies; previous work experience that may not be directly applicable; hesitation to take a proactive stance in their job search; and visa limitations regarding the amount of time they are permitted to work. In the United States as elsewhere, there are many companies that will not pay for the legal costs of obtaining a visa that permits a nonpermanent resident to work. Obtaining a summer internship may also present challenges to international students since many large U.S. corporations view summer interns as potential future employees. If a company has a policy of not hiring individuals without residency permits, it may also choose not to hire F-1 or J-1 visa holders as interns.

While many talented international students find summer internships in the United States and very good permanent jobs following graduation from MBA programs, career services professionals often find that even the most accomplished international students may hesitate to be as proactive in their job searches as the typical U.S. student. International students who are "career changers" and wish to work in the United States encounter even greater placement challenges because they face all of the hurdles confronting domestic "career changers" as well as the issues already listed.

Understanding placement concerns that may affect the way in which admissions and career services staff analyze international students' stated career goals will help you to address these issues in your application. A convincing essay about your career goals, therefore, requires substantive explanations of how you plan to leverage your past experience and your future MBA education to obtain the type of job you want.

Two final pieces of advice after completing your application: Keep copies of all forms you send to each school and check to make sure that all references to the school are consistent within each application. Admissions committees realize that nearly all candidates will apply to at least several MBA programs; however, you can damage a carefully crafted impression by referring to School X in your essays or cover letters for School Y.

Analyzing Your Statistical Profile

When you read about a specific school, make sure to review the profile of accepted applicants and compare it to your own background. School profiles usually include statistics on average grades in university courses, average or minimum GMAT and TOEFL scores, and average years of postuniversity full-time work experience. Only after gaining an accurate understanding of the profile of accepted candidates and the distinctive features of your targeted business schools can you write an application in which you can "sell yourself" effectively to a school's admissions committee.

As you analyze the profiles of accepted students at your targeted schools, be advised that in many highly competitive schools there are many more qualified applicants than available places. Therefore, it is a good strategy to apply to at least three or four schools. If your credentials are below the stated average in any area noted in a school's profile, you may want to take advantage of the optional essay (discussed in the preceding section on essays) to explain your particular situation. If your qualifications are lower than those of accepted students on all scales or are significantly below the stated averages in one or more of the categories, you may not have a realistic chance of being accepted. As shown in Table 5.1, neither fictional candidate is likely to be admitted to School X. Applicant A is below average on all quantifiable criteria, while Applicant B's standardized test scores are probably sufficiently low to prohibit admission.

If you are in doubt about your chances of being accepted to a school in which you have a strong interest, apply anyway; however, if your primary goal is to attend an MBA program, then also apply to schools where you have a realistic chance of being accepted.

When you have thoroughly researched your target schools and matched your own profile to that of recently accepted students, you

*Table 5.1   Comparison of Accepted Students and Applicants at
               School X*

	Profile of Accepted Students	Profile of Applicant A	Profile of Applicant B
Average years full-time work	4.5	2.0	7.0
Average GMAT/ minimum AWA	625/3.5	550/3.0	480/2.5
Minimum TOEFL/ minimum TWE	600/4.0	570/3.5	550/3.0
Grade-point average	3.3	2.9	3.4

are ready to face what may be the most challenging issue: a realistic
assessment of your skills in English.

How English Skills Are Evaluated by Admissions Officers and How to Improve Your Current Skills

Admissions committees know that graduate business courses require
a great deal of reading, writing, and class and group participation.
Therefore, every international application is carefully scrutinized for
evidence that a candidate's skills in English can meet the demands of
a particular MBA program.

Participating in Class

Class participation is central to pedagogy in U.S. MBA programs;
MBA faculty members believe that learning is accelerated when
students are actively engaged in sharing and defending their ideas,
challenging the opinions of others, and comparing previous business
and life experiences. Professors and students alike are eager to hear
the perspectives of international participants and can become
frustrated when international students are silent during discussions,
communicate with great difficulty, or socialize nearly exclusively with
people from their native countries and regions. To reinforce the

importance of total class participation and group work, most MBA professors incorporate an assessment of class participation into their grade determinations.

Admissions officers use multiple criteria to evaluate a candidate's ability to use English proficiently and to become an active member of the school community:

- the verbal score on and essay from the GMAT

- the AWA (Analytical Writing Assessment) score and essays

- TOEFL and TWE scores

- comments made in letters of recommendation

- essays (writing style and content as compared to writing samples included in the AWA section of the GMAT)

- correspondence by letter and e-mail

- interviews in English, either in person or by telephone

- previous course work in English

Admissions readers look carefully at all of these areas, seeking evidence that prospective students will participate in fast-paced class discussions, small group meetings, and nonacademic MBA activities such as clubs, support groups, and student government. In addition to evaluating English skills, admissions committees try to determine whether international applicants are likely to play active roles in the MBA community.

Admissions committees also recognize that the level of participation expected and even demanded in U.S. MBA programs—such as speaking in public, questioning the opinions of professors and colleagues, and arguing with peers—may be the opposite of what is considered acceptable and polite in other cultures. They also know that candidates who are extremely shy or who refrain from expressing personal opinions—either because of weak English skills or particular cultural backgrounds—may have a hard time fitting into and contributing to the learning communities of U.S. MBA programs. Therefore, while trying to be sensitive to the different cultural and behavioral practices and beliefs of other countries, MBA admissions committees seek out students who can both benefit from and contribute to the MBA community and learning environment.

Improving Your English Skills

How can international applicants improve their ability to communicate effectively in English? What follows are a few of the many ways to strengthen your English skills as you first prepare to take the TOEFL and GMAT exams and then look ahead to life as a student in a U.S. MBA program:

- Enroll for several months in an intensive English program in the United States prior to starting the MBA application process.

- Schedule English "conversation sessions" with a native English speaker at least twice each week for thirty to sixty minutes.

- Read business magazines and newspapers, such as *The Wall Street Journal, Business Week, Fortune,* and *Forbes.* Ask colleagues competent in English to explain difficult terms.

- "Surf" the Web, reading through the Web sites of many different schools.

- Listen regularly to English-language television and radio programs, repeating aloud selected lines of dialogue.

Focusing on Conversational English

Of all the suggestions mentioned, practicing English with native English speakers is probably the most valuable. Unfortunately, some applicants focus on either repeatedly taking the TOEFL or TOEFL preparation courses because, as some candidates have explained, they "did not have the time to attend conversation classes." This strategy can backfire during an interview when the candidate is unable to engage in a fluent conversation. You might title your conversation program "What do you think of . . . ?" to prepare yourself mentally for interactive MBA classes in which you will be asked to give your opinion. Base each meeting on a topic covered in a short English-language newspaper or magazine article. To gain the greatest benefit from English conversation sessions, it is best to schedule a larger number of short meetings each week than to hold one long session.

Preprogram English Courses

Preprogram English courses are offered at colleges, universities, and for-profit, independent schools throughout the United States. To select the program that best suits your needs, speak with the admissions offices of schools you hope to attend as well as with friends and colleagues who have enrolled in such programs.

Many MBA programs accept international applicants with the requirement that they come to the United States before the start of their program to attend intensive English preparation courses. Recommendations regarding the length and type of courses are based on evaluations of TOEFL and GMAT performance, essays, and interaction in face-to-face or telephone interviews. Some schools offer a "conditional acceptance," which requires prospective students to attain a targeted level of competence in English or a specific TOEFL score before they are officially accepted.

Services to Support Writing on Campus

Nearly all MBA programs require a large amount of written work. To support this activity, students use a variety of campus resources. Some schools have English as a Second Language (ESL) programs on campus. Many MBA programs sponsor free writing centers through which students can get help on a variety of writing projects including drafting and revising cover letters and resumes, documents used in presentations, papers, and memos. In most cases, the function of writing center staff is to correct grammatical errors and point out passages that are unclear or unfocused. Rewriting entire assignments is not the proper role of writing center assistants. Therefore, students with weak skills in written English should strongly consider attending intensive English writing courses before enrolling in their MBA programs.

Financing Your MBA, Financial Aid, and Assistantships

Before a school can issue an IAP-66 or I-20 student visa invitation (leading to an F-1 or J-1 student visa), the U.S. government requires international students to provide the school with a number of documents, including those that certify adequate funds for financing the students' education. Funds can come from several sources: government or private foundations in the student's home country; public or privately supported funds from U.S. sources; a scholarship and/or assistantship from the MBA school; and private resources, including funds from the student's own savings (since many MBA students have worked for a number of years), the student's parents, or other family members.

Verifying Funding

Many schools include in their application packet a Financial Certificate which outlines financial requirements for attending the MBA program. This document requires you to certify the availability of funds to ensure that all expenses will be covered during the time you are pursuing your MBA. The certificate lists the real costs of books, housing, and health insurance at the school; figures for food and living expenses are supplied by the U.S. Department of Labor for the city in which the MBA program is located. Items that are listed on the Financial Certificate include the following:

- tuition and fees
- housing
- food
- living expenses, including apartment setup costs
- health insurance
- books and supplies

No visa invitation can be issued until you sign this certificate and accompanying documents and send them back to the school. Most schools require that students supply original documents from banks and funding agencies that guarantee the availability of funds. In some countries, the U.S. Embassy will look more favorably on the request for a student visa if the full amount of funding required for one or both years has been transferred to the student's account in the MBA school. Students should check with the MBA program offices of the schools they plan to attend to learn if it is required or desirable to transfer funds after their acceptance and before applying for the student visa.

Financial Aid

The availability of financial aid varies greatly among MBA programs throughout the United States. Many programs do not offer aid to international students. Financial aid is actually composed of two different sources:

- Tuition scholarships are outright financial awards that do not need to be repaid and are awarded based on need, merit, or both.

- Graduate or teaching assistantships require the recipient to work in return for a fixed or hourly salary.

Some programs offer both types of financial assistance. While some competitive MBA schools have extensive scholarship programs, many others offer neither scholarships nor guaranteed assistantships to international students. Each school sets its own rules and standards regarding how aid is awarded and whether a separate aid application is required; you must understand all criteria and standards so that you can make an effective application for tuition scholarship. If your targeted schools do not provide a separate financial aid form, you should feel free to write the admissions committee a letter noting your interest in being considered for financial aid.

Many scholarships offered at the graduate level are based solely on merit (which helps schools attract particularly gifted students) or on a combination of merit and financial need. To be reviewed for the financial awards that are available to international students, it is critically important that you send in your application by the stated deadline. When scholarships are offered, the conditions under which funds are awarded include guaranteeing the same level of scholarship support for the entire MBA program, regardless of grades; requiring the student to maintain a specific grade-point average (often a B or better); or guaranteeing tuition scholarship for the first year only.

After determining if a school offers financial aid to international students, you must carefully evaluate the school's profile of accepted students. If you have higher grades and test scores and longer work experience than the averages outlined in the school's profile, you may have a good chance of receiving some tuition scholarship funding. If you come from a significantly underrepresented part of the world and your profile is nearly identical to the profile of the most recent entering class, you may also have a chance of being seriously considered for financial aid. The weaker your statistical profile is in comparison to that outlined for the previous year's accepted class, the weaker your chance of receiving a tuition scholarship.

Assistantships

Graduate and teaching assistantships also vary greatly from one institution to another. Most universities have some form of assistantship through which students may work on campus with professors or in university or business school offices. Throughout the United States, pay rates vary widely, as do the number of hours students are asked to devote to assistantship work. Students with F-1 visas get permission to work on campus directly from the school's foreign student advisor, and J-1 visa holders usually have no problem getting permission from their visa issuers to accept on-campus, business-related jobs.

In many schools, international students are urged to work no more than ten to twelve hours per week during the first semester so that they can adjust to life in the United States and the demanding MBA workload. By the second semester, some students can work fifteen hours per week and still devote sufficient time to their course work and school activities. In the second year, some students work as many as twenty hours per week, while others cut back as they realize that planning and executing an active search for a permanent job can take as much time and energy as preparing for an additional course. Even if you must work to support yourself, remember that professors expect that your first priority is to classes, outside preparation, and team meetings.

Getting Ready to Start Your MBA Program

Before coming to the United States you will undoubtedly have many specific questions about three critical nonacademic issues: securing your visa, obtaining health insurance, and finding housing. You will also need to decide when to schedule your arrival and what to bring with you for your long stay away from home.

Getting Your Visa

Several months before you are scheduled to arrive in the United States, your MBA program will send you information about getting your student visa. As described at the beginning of this chapter, the I-20 or IAP-66 visa invitation issued by your school permits you to go to a U.S. Embassy or consulate to get an F-1 or J-1 student visa.

If you plan to attend a language program in the United States before enrolling in your MBA program, the language program must issue its own visa invitation covering the time you will spend there. Under this circumstance, you should explain your plans to both the language program and the MBA program to make sure that your visas are complementary and allow you to remain in the United States without returning home between your language training and the start of your MBA program. This coordination will ensure that you are in compliance with U.S. visa regulations.

Health Insurance

Most U.S. universities require international students to have health insurance in order to enroll in their academic programs; however, the specific categories and levels of coverage vary from one school to another. In order to remain in good standing, international students must comply with the type and level of coverage mandated by the school in which they enroll.

The simplest way to obtain the required level of health insurance is to buy the policy recommended by your school. If your government or your parents provide comprehensive health insurance, you must send an English-language version of the policy to the appropriate university officer to determine whether your policy provides coverage at the level required by the university. If your existing policy is approved, do not forget to bring an original copy of your insurance card. Once you are enrolled in your MBA program, you may learn about a less expensive policy that offers identical coverage. If you wish, and in consultation with the school's designated health insurance advisor, you may change policies.

Having good medical insurance and maintaining continuous coverage throughout your stay in the United States are critical to your health and your financial well-being, for while medical treatment in the United States is often superb, it is very expensive. If you face a medical emergency for which you do not have proper insurance, your choices of treatment, hospitals, and doctors may be limited. Medical insurance is not designed to cover all costs associated with medical care or every type of medical problem. Instead, a good insurance policy will protect students from paying large amounts of money to treat major medical problems that might require a hospital stay or long-term doctor's care. Under most policies, the student is responsible for paying a portion of doctors' bills and hospital stays. Some universities provide very good coverage through on-campus clinics that can treat routine medical problems. Preventive and routine dental care are usually excluded from general health insurance policies.

It is strongly recommended that you (1) maintain continuous coverage during your entire stay in the United States; (2) read your policy carefully to understand exactly what is covered and what you are responsible for paying; and (3) ask questions if you are ever in doubt about anything regarding your policy and your coverage.

Housing

Many U.S. universities have university housing. However, in large urban areas the number of apartments that are available may be very limited. Monthly housing prices vary greatly from one area of the country to another, and your best source of information will be your school's admissions or international student office. Some schools may offer to send you guidebooks on renting local apartments and provide you with lists of students looking for roommates. University housing offices in suburban or rural areas often maintain lists of houses for rent where a family or several students can live together. Some campuses make such lists available at their Web sites.

University housing has many advantages for international students: It is often less expensive than open market rental housing; it is usually close to campus; most units are furnished; and you may not need to pay up-front deposits for rent and utilities. Other amenities may include on-site laundry facilities, a computer lab, free local telephone lines, and free shuttle bus service to campus and nearby shopping.

One drawback to campus housing is that it can be older and less luxurious than other apartments in the community. Renting on the open market, in contrast, gives you access to all types of housing but will probably carry with it the added financial burden of having to pay deposits for rent, gas, and electricity. *A final caution:* If you do not plan to buy a car as soon as you arrive, make sure that your housing has good access to public transportation. Public transportation, especially in suburban or rural areas and in the South, is much less frequent and reliable than in major cities in the rest of the world. (There is more information on driving and transportation in the last section of this chapter.)

If you plan to arrive at your school without housing, make reservations to stay in a nearby hotel for about one week, since this is usually the average amount of time required for finding an apartment and getting basic furniture.

Deciding What to Bring with You

You will not have unlimited space in your luggage, but it is often less expensive to pay an excess baggage charge to the airlines than to buy the items in the United States. Check with the airlines on their excess baggage policy and review carefully what you will need. Here are some of the key items to consider bringing with you:

- **Money and credit cards** It is strongly recommended that you bring cash or U.S. denomination traveler's checks with you. It is also very useful to bring a credit card such as Visa, MasterCard, or American Express. If you are from a country with a nonconvertible currency, you will need to bring your money in U.S. dollars or traveler's checks.

One large southern university recommends that students bring $1,000 to $1,500 in cash to pay for initial expenses such as food, deposits for an apartment or utilities, health insurance, books, and supplies. Within several days of arrival, you will want to open a bank account (a simple procedure in the United States) so that you can deposit excess cash and receive transfers of funds from home. If you bring hard currency, you can exchange it at an airport upon arrival (check to see when the currency exchange windows are open if you arrive before 9:00 A.M. or after 7:00 P.M.). Domestic U.S. train and bus stations do not have currency changing facilities.

- **Computers** Given the strong emphasis on technology at all U.S. universities, it is recommended that you bring a computer if you have one. Even though you will have access to a university and/or business school computer center, having your own computer is a great advantage in getting your work done. If you do not own a computer or if your computer is relatively old, you may want to wait until you get to the United States to buy one. Prices for hardware and software are very competitive, and many stores and universities offer significant discounts.

    Even if your school does not require that you own a computer, we strongly suggest that you either bring a laptop or plan to buy a computer at the beginning of your program. Prior to arriving at your MBA program, make sure that you understand computer competency standards as well as minimum computer configurations recommended by your MBA program so that you can master required skills and determine if your current machine is adequate.

- **Clothes** In most U.S. business school classes, students will feel comfortable wearing casual clothes, including shorts and jeans; women often wear slacks to class. Appropriate dress for business meetings (called *business attire* in many MBA catalogs) will be needed from the beginning of the first semester for your own in-class presentations, meeting members of the business community, internships, and job interviews. Business attire is typically defined as a suit and tie for men and a suit for women. Unless you have previously worked in the United States, take time to observe attire in formal business settings before making your own personal style decisions. Normally, wearing a dark suit is a safe option.

The climate of the city where your program is located will dictate the nature of the clothing you should bring. Even in some southern states there can be relatively cold weather (occasionally minus 5 degrees to 5 degrees Centigrade) from late November through early February. Therefore, if you will attend a school in the southern United States, you should bring winter clothes such as sweaters, long-sleeved shirts, wool or other heavyweight pants and suits, a heavy jacket and/or coat, gloves, hat, and a scarf. Temperatures in the Northeast, Northwest, or Midwest—while well below freezing in the winter months—may be very warm during the fall and early summer, occasionally rising to between 28 degrees and 32 degrees Centigrade.

If you enjoy athletic activities, don't forget your sneakers or training shoes, golf clubs, tennis racket, swimsuit, and other sports-related clothing and equipment. Many U.S. schools have superb athletic facilities with free access for students. Most schools also have tennis courts on campus and many are located near public golf courses.

Finally, you may want to bring clothes you would wear to a formal party in your own country, including any clothing that is native to your country, because some schools hold formal dances or cultural festivals each year.

- **Items for your apartment** You can easily buy inexpensive pots and pans, cutlery, plates, cups and glasses, bedding, towels, and other small items for your apartment. If you want to save some money, consider bringing some unbreakable items with you. To remind you of home, you may want to bring photographs or small pictures as well as posters that you may be able to find at a sales office of your country's national airline.

- **Musical instruments and cultural artifacts** Music can be a wonderful way to meet people, and many parties take on new life when guitars appear and participants begin to sing. Portable musical instruments, "native" clothes, and other items from your home country are welcome additions to the global festivals and other cultural programs that are held in many schools. Also bring recipes for your favorite foods so you can cook meals you enjoy and share your food and traditions with new friends from around the world.

Scheduling Your Arrival

Before making airline reservations, you will want to gather a lot of information. What follows are some of the specific questions to ask, if answers are not provided in the prearrival guide sent to you by your MBA program:

- What is the optimal time to arrive at your school? Consider all preprogram activities before making this decision.
- When should you inform the school of your arrival date?
- Which airport should you use? Will anyone meet you?
- What are the schedules and costs of ground transportation needed to get to campus?
- What are the business hours of the university office?
- Where should you stay for your first several nights?
- Who should you contact if you have a travel emergency?

An important suggestion: Pack in your carry-on baggage the telephone numbers for your key contacts so you can make a call if you face any problems upon arrival.

Getting Settled

When you arrive at either your English program or your MBA school, you should first check in with the admissions or international program office. Within two days, you should present your papers (visa, passport, and so on) to the university office responsible for international students.
  Next, there are several tasks that you should do:

- Find or confirm your housing and register for utilities.
- Open a bank account, a simple procedure. You may need to show proof of residency, such as an apartment lease.
- Buy basic kitchen or bathroom items for your apartment.
- Buy or rent furniture. Yes, stores in some U.S. cities rent furniture!

- Familiarize yourself with campus so you can start to feel comfortable with your surroundings.

Once you have settled into your new home and are starting to feel comfortable on campus, it is time to turn your attention to your academic program.

The Academic Environment and What Is Expected of You

This section focuses on many of the important issues that underlie the academic environment you are about to enter: faculty accessibility, diverse teaching styles, class participation, teamwork, asking for help, and the Academic Honor Code. Although some of the information outlined next may be familiar to you, it is more than likely that the norms of behavior and academic expectations discussed here are very different from what you have experienced in non-U.S. educational institutions and in your university-level education. Confronting these issues now will give you a head start in understanding the academic environment you are about to enter, which in turn will help you derive maximum benefit from your MBA experience.

To gain a deeper understanding of the key aspects of MBA academic life in the United States, read this information carefully and then talk with friends and colleagues who are attending U.S. MBA programs about their perceptions of academic life and MBA culture before you arrive.

Getting to Know Faculty and Staff Members at Your School

One of the reasons students choose to attend a specific institution is because of the quality and reputation of the faculty. All too frequently, however, students (and particularly international students) do not take advantage of this valuable resource. While it is true that some faculty members are more approachable than others and some professors in large research universities may not devote much out-of-classroom time to MBA students, there are many professors who thoroughly enjoy contact with students and are great sources of advice, support, and job connections. Staff members in admissions, career services, international programs, and student services also have valuable insights and alumni contacts that they will be happy to share with you.

Faculty members usually include their office telephone numbers and office hours on their course syllabi as a way to encourage students to see them during the semester. E-mail provides another convenient way to contact faculty. Some international students hesitate to e-mail faculty members before first meeting them, because in their cultures it is necessary either to arrange a meeting in person or, at the very least, to have a phone conversation that sets the meeting time. In the United States, faculty are very accustomed to receiving e-mails as first points of contact.

Diverse Teaching Styles

As noted in Chapter 3, a few schools (Harvard and the Darden School at the University of Virginia, for example) rely exclusively on a single teaching method. Most schools, however, encourage their faculty to use the teaching techniques—including case study, lecture/discussion, group projects, and simulations—the faculty consider to be most effective. By and large, faculty in marketing and management make greater use of case studies and small-group work, while faculty teaching quantitative courses such as accounting, finance, and statistics rely more heavily on lecture/discussion and individual tests. However, you should not be surprised to have case discussions and group work in some, perhaps many, of your quantitative courses. Most professors expect some degree of class participation, although not all faculty members give grades for participation.

Think of the faculty and staff at your business school as important sources of information who can become key members of your future worldwide, professional network. Do not allow yourself to graduate wishing you had made contact with a professor or staff member but having failed to do so out of shyness or lack of initiative. Be proactive (just as in class participation) and find a way to talk with the people you want to meet. You will always be glad that you made the effort.

More on Student-Centered Learning and Class Participation

As you may already know, U.S. MBA programs place great emphasis on participation in class. Participation is not restricted to "case" classes, in which all or most of the work is based on case studies, and the importance of participation is often reinforced when professors assign a significant percentage of a student's grade to the quality and/or quantity of comments he or she made in class.

Professors and administrators realize that it may be very difficult for international students to state and defend their opinions in a second language. Some professors try to help international students ease into making their first comments in class, while others make no allowances for international participants, treating them exactly as they treat all other students. In any case, the responsibility for performance in courses clearly rests on the shoulders of each student, international or domestic.

Sometimes, international students express the opinion that being graded on class participation in the same way as their U.S. classmates is "unfair." Few schools (or international students), however, would want to establish a two-tiered grading system that would lead to two classifications of MBA students, generating the possibility that one group might be viewed as being of a lesser quality than the other. With class participation, as with adjusting to the norms of the academic environment in U.S. MBA programs, the issue is not one of fairness; it is about understanding what lies at the heart of the student-centered approach to learning that has been adopted by U.S. MBA programs.

What will happen if you are slow to participate, perhaps waiting until the second semester to venture a comment in class? There are several straightforward consequences, besides the risk of a lower grade: You will learn less, your classmates will learn less, your teachers will miss your contributions, and you will feel less a part of the MBA community.

Student-centered learning views students as central to the education process and requires that they become active participants who take responsibility for their own education. The need for students to be proactive permeates all aspects of academic life—in and out of the classroom, in contacts among students, and in internship and job searches. A central reason that MBA programs place such emphasis on class participation is the strong belief that managers in business can perform well in their jobs only by taking the initiative and shouldering decision-making responsibility. In addition, communication skills are usually a key factor in effective performance in business. In some countries, following the lead of a senior manager or keeping opinions to oneself are honorable and appropriate business behaviors. In most U.S. businesses, where seniority is not necessarily the key to promotion, such "passive" behavior could be a prescription for losing opportunities and, perhaps, your job.

Because the emphasis on participation is likely to be very different from what you have experienced in your previous education, it is wise to prepare yourself mentally to participate in your courses long before the start of your MBA program. How can you approach this challenging task? A number of techniques can help you "break the ice" and find ways to begin participating in your classes.

One highly effective strategy is to discuss the key issues in a case study with a small group of classmates prior to each class. In this way, you can practice expressing your ideas aloud; then, if any of your points arise during class discussion, you can quickly raise your hand and offer your input.

Visit your faculty members in their offices to express your interest in participating and to seek their advice on how to begin. Be open about why it is hard for you to speak up in class and discuss ways you might become more comfortable making comments. Most faculty members react very positively when students speak with them directly about the problems they are experiencing. Professors view a visit from a student as an expression of interest in their course and regard the student's initiative in tackling difficult issues as an indication of willingness to take responsibility.

The following techniques, devised by international students, have helped them ease into class participation. Ask your professors to

- call on you to answer the first question of the class, which in a case class is often a request to describe the important elements of the case under discussion.

- call on you directly, even when your hand is not raised.

- consider counting comments you make in the course conference on the school's intranet system as class participation.

Teamwork

Case studies, projects, and simulations all require students to work in teams. Even some lecture/discussion classes may involve a group presentation. Be aware that in the United States, the usual way of dividing up work in a small group is for each team member to volunteer to do that part of the work that is most suitable or interesting to him or her. If group activity in your culture means waiting to be assigned your portion of the project, you may find yourself doing the one piece of work that no one else wants. Learning to take a proactive stance while working with classmates from different cultural, academic, ethnic, and professional backgrounds may be challenging at first. However, as you work with your diverse classmates within the MBA environment and the dominant U.S. culture, you will form your own conclusions on how to accomplish the groups' goals while using the talents of all members.

The way that teams are formed varies from one school to another. In some MBA programs, you may have a single study group or team for all of your courses during the first semester; in other schools, you may be part of a different team in every class. Some professors or administrators may assign students to teams while other professors will tell the class members to form their own teams—at which point you must be prepared to work actively to become part of a team of classmates with whom you want to work.

Do not "hang back" and sit silently when your groups meet. Prepare for group meetings so that you can not only express your opinion on the direction the project should take, but also volunteer to do that portion of the project that is of greatest interest to you. By not speaking up, you may inadvertently give the impression that you cannot or do not want to do your fair share of the work.

Asking for Help

One of the most critical skills to learn while in your MBA program is knowing when and how to ask for help. This skill, another example of taking responsibility for your own learning, poses some particularly thorny problems for international students. The key to asking for help is, of course, to recognize that you need help. This may be very difficult to accept for many reasons: if you have always been a top student, if you were one of a small number of employees selected by your company to attend an MBA program, if your family and friends are financing your education at great personal cost to themselves, or if asking for help in your culture is an admission of failure. In the United States, however, asking for help is often interpreted in a very positive way: You are commended for analyzing your situation and for your proactive decision to seek advice.

During general orientation, MBA program directors and international student advisors repeatedly say that the main problem students face in asking for help is waiting too long before seeking help. If you wait too long, a problem can become a full-blown crisis and options can become extremely limited. Of course, all students should first try to solve problems by themselves; however, if they have spent far more time than their colleagues, tried every conceivable solution, and are still far from overcoming a problem, it is clearly time to seek outside help.

If you know that you need an outside opinion to solve a difficult academic or personal problem, discuss that problem with the person at your school with whom you feel most comfortable. During an initial meeting you may learn of ways to handle your problem that you had never imagined. What you may have regarded as an unsolvable crisis may be a situation your advisor has seen many times before and for which there is a ready solution.

Academic Honor Code

All U.S. schools are governed by the Academic Honor Code, a written document that describes the behavior each community expects of its members with respect to academic work; the code also defines ways in which the norms of academic conduct can be violated. Usually, a copy of the honor code is given to all students at the general MBA orientation. In many schools, there is an honor council composed of students or students and faculty members that reviews violations of the code. A distinctive feature of most honor codes in U.S. universities is that all members of the academic community are responsible for upholding the rules and values of the community. If, for example, people witness an honor code violation, such as cheating on an exam, the code requires that they report the violation; to watch silently and do nothing is also considered a violation of the code because it is viewed as a failure to uphold the accepted rules of fairness that govern the community.

One of the most common violations of the honor code involves plagiarism, which is defined as using someone else's words or ideas without giving full and proper credit. One of the most common forms of plagiarism is reproducing a part of a book or article in a document without acknowledging the name of the source and the location of the idea or concept.

In business school, there is another type of plagiarism that can arise from a misunderstanding of where consultation ends and individual work begins. One example of potentially inadvertent plagiarism can arise during preparation for take-home exams, which students must write without supervision and within a specific time limit using the sources permitted by the professor. There can be instances in which a professor permits students to discuss all aspects of the course as a means of reviewing for the exam but does not permit explicit discussion of the exam questions. Under these circumstances, it is possible for friends to discuss and debate topics so close to the exam question that they "cross the line" between general discussion and issues to be addressed on the exam question itself. Also, if students study together throughout the semester, they could write very similar take-home exams even if they do not discuss any issues related to the exam question. As with so many other issues, the way to ensure that you work within the guidelines and expectations of your MBA program is to ask questions if you have any doubts about what you should do.

Preparing to Begin Your MBA Program

To help orient and prepare students to perform at a high level from the moment regular classes begin, most U.S. MBA programs offer a variety of preprogram activities including academic short courses and a general orientation. Many universities also offer programs designed especially for incoming international students such as all-university international orientations, international MBA orientations, special short courses in English and U.S. culture, and introductions to case study classes.

Academic Preprogram Short Courses

Many schools offer a variety of preprogram short courses that are open to all incoming students and may include accounting, math review, and statistics. As a condition of your admission, you may be required to take some or all of these courses. Even if you are not required to take the courses, you may choose to enroll as a way to "tune" your ears to hearing technical vocabulary in English and to experience life in a U.S. classroom without the stress of grades. Often, there is a separate charge for these preprogram classes.

If you are unsure about whether to take any of the preprogram academic courses at your MBA school, discuss the issue with the admissions office.

Orientations

Orientations are designed to provide information about all aspects of your MBA program to help you meet your own goals and those of the school. All students are required to attend the general MBA orientation, which normally lasts for three to seven days prior to registration. At the general orientation, business school staff, faculty, and students will cover all or most of the following topics:

- a profile of your classmates

- an introduction to faculty and their expectations of students

- the curriculum and special academic programs

- academic advising

- the grading system

- the Academic Honor Code

- clubs and other extracurricular activities

- the career services office and job-search services

An international MBA orientation, which is held at many schools, usually lasts for either a half or full day and is often held shortly before the general orientation begins. Normally, international students are expected to attend both the general and the international MBA orientations.

Academic Advising

To help you construct an academic schedule that meets your needs and takes into account the skills you already possess, you will work with an academic advisor. Before registration day, you will be assigned to an academic advisor. Each school maintains its own method of academic advising, so your advisor may be a professor, a staff director of academic advising, a member of the MBA program office, or a combination of these individuals. You can also consult with the school's director of international programs or foreign student advisor as well as with professors in your special fields of interest as you progress through your MBA program. In this way, you will gain additional perspectives and take full advantage of the school's offerings.

Waiving Core Courses

All MBA programs include core (required foundation) courses and electives. If you already have substantial background in one or more core subjects—such as accounting, economics, finance, marketing, and statistics—you may be able to "waive" one or more core courses. (*Waiving* a course means being released from the requirement of taking it by demonstrating that you know nearly all of the material to be covered.) A waiver exam, one method used to determine your proficiency in a particular subject, is created and graded by a professor responsible for the introductory course you wish to waive. Some schools send sample waiver exams to students during the several months prior to the start of school so they can understand the scope of material to be covered in each core course. The exams are usually administered before classes begin so that students can learn the results before finalizing their first-semester schedules.

In some schools, waiving a core course enables you to reduce the total number of classes you are required to take; in others, you must enroll in the same number of credit hours to graduate but you may take electives in place of the waived core courses.

Registration Day

On registration day, you will probably be asked to pay for your health insurance, tuition, and fees (unless you have sent the payments before your arrival at school), and you should receive your student identification (I.D.) card. Now your life as an MBA student is really ready to begin!

Life in the United States

If you come to the United States to attend an MBA program, you are undoubtedly prepared to spend a great deal of time studying and mastering business skills. It is clear that you not only value the educational opportunities in the United States but also wish to learn about life and culture in a foreign country while making new friends. Adjusting to life in here will be exhilarating and frustrating, enjoyable and challenging, the source of tension and of great pride. To prepare for this memorable experience, review the following insights on some of the areas of greatest interest to international students.

Shopping for Food and Eating Out

Even if you live in a small city, you will be able to find food stores that are open throughout the day. In large cities, it is common to find twenty-four-hour supermarkets that sell not only food but also magazines, cleaning products, pharmaceuticals, and many other products. In some states, wine and beer are also sold in supermarkets.

In small cities or rural areas, it may be difficult to locate fresh fruits and vegetables or canned goods that you are accustomed to purchasing at home. To find familiar foods, contact people from your country who are already enrolled in the school you will attend to ask about where they shop. Mail-order companies can supply spices and canned goods, and trips to larger cities nearby will likely permit you to stock up on the fruits and vegetables you miss from home.

One of the biggest adjustments faced by international students is to the food in university cafeterias, which may be very different than that found in many parts of the world, especially Asia. Depending on your budget, your culinary tastes, and your willingness to cook, you may need to develop a taste for new foods. Another major adjustment for many international male students is learning to cook. Overcoming the challenge may prove very worthwhile, for many students find that cooking and sharing food is a way to re-create the flavors of home as well as make new friends from all over the world.

In many MBA programs, students are so busy that they often go to the university cafeteria or inexpensive, nearby restaurants to eat quick lunches and dinners. In most U.S. cities, you will find many different types of restaurants offering a wide variety of choices: fast-food restaurants (including McDonald's, Burger King, and Kentucky Fried Chicken); home-style or gourmet restaurants (including those offering the food of China, Japan, Mexico, France, Thailand, and India); and regional U.S. restaurants (featuring barbecue, New Orleans Cajun, or TexMex cuisine, for example). Restaurant costs vary widely from about $5 for a meal in a fast-food restaurant to over $100 per person in a high-quality gourmet restaurant.

Driving and Transportation

If you have a driver's license, remember to bring it with you. Even if you don't plan to buy or rent a car, getting a U.S. driver's license or identity card is important so you can write bank checks and so you do not have to carry a large amount of cash with you. Although your passport is an identity document that enables the U.S. government to track your movement across international borders, it is seldom accepted as a form of identification when you want to write a check because it lists no place of residence in the United States.

Many students who come to the United States for graduate school consider buying used cars for use during their stays. In the larger cities in the Midwest and Northeast—such as Boston, Chicago, New York, Philadelphia, and Washington, D.C.—this may not be a wise economic decision because parking is very costly, finding a parking spot is very difficult, and parking tickets are very expensive. In cities in which the public transportation system is good, doing without a car most of the time and renting a car for week or weekend trips is by far the cheapest and easiest way to travel.

However, in the rest of the country, the transportation situation is different. In parts of the Southeast, Southwest, Plains States, West, Northeast, and Northwest, there are large distances to travel within metropolitan areas and extremely long distances to travel between cities. In the cities that do not have well-developed public transportation systems, the wait for a bus, train, or metro (subway) is much longer than it is in most large cities in the rest of the world, and service sometimes ends as early as 9:00 P.M. As a result, shortly after arrival many international students decide to buy new or used cars, either by themselves or with newly made friends. The cost of used cars varies widely, but in some parts of the United States it is possible to buy a reliable used car for between $2,000 and $5,000. Insurance is required and is an extra cost.

International students should not feel compelled to buy cars. U.S. students who do not own cars often ask others for rides, so even in the areas of the country known for their "car cultures," international students should not hesitate to ask classmates for rides home after late night group meetings, study sessions at the library, or parties.

Social Life and Getting to Know U.S. Students

There are many opportunities to meet your classmates outside of class. The student services offices of many business schools regularly sponsor morning coffee hours or other programs at which students, faculty, and staff mingle over coffee and donuts. In some schools, the student government or clubs organize Thursday or Friday evening social gatherings on campus, in local clubs or restaurants, or in students' apartments. On many campuses, university-wide international students offices sponsor weekly lunches or coffee hours and welcome international students from all divisions of the university.

Business school student groups may also sponsor a variety of popular events such as international dinners (to which all students contribute "native" dishes), international restaurant evenings, or global festivals. These kinds of programs often attract U.S. students and faculty eager to taste the cooking of other countries and learn more about the cultures of international participants.

In many cultures, the arrangement of social meetings (familiarly called "dates") is done with much more advance notice than in the

United States. As a result, many international students may feel uncomfortable when they are asked to participate in a gathering or go to dinner with only a few days' (or hours') advance notice. In contrast, U.S. students tend to be very informal about arranging times to meet with their friends, often deciding only hours before an event if they want to attend. This pattern is especially true of busy MBA students who ration their free time and often cannot predict when they will complete their class assignments. Given the informality and last-minute nature of many social interactions, international students need to be proactive in establishing relationships with their U.S. classmates, just as in class participation and job search.

Many U.S. students are likely to invite international students to join them for meals, movies, or other events at the beginning of the academic year, but after the first several weeks, a large number of these same students will not go out of their way to extend invitations to international students. Just like you, U.S. students will be very busy, consumed by the demands of their courses, extracurricular activities, and internship or job searches. Therefore, if you want to spend more time with your U.S. classmates outside of class, you may need to take the initiative. Consider asking them to do the following:

- have coffee or a meal during the school day
- go to a movie, concert, or play
- travel to a park or historic site on a weekend
- come to your home for dinner

If the first—or even the second and third—person you invite is unable to accept, don't be hurt or discouraged; instead, accept the response and move on to the next person on your list. Even if your classmates cannot accept your invitation for one occasion, they will be flattered to have been asked.

Conclusion

Attending school in another country provides a magnificent opportunity to stretch yourself to the limits of your abilities. Regardless of which MBA program you select, you will return home a changed person because the experience of living and working in another country will give you a fresh perspective on yourself, your own country, and your career. By overcoming obstacles, facing new challenges, adjusting expectations, and working very hard, you will acquire new skills, establish an international network of friends and business colleagues, and give yourself a tremendous competitive edge in managing your life and future career.

6

Admissions Criteria

Is your undergraduate grade point not what it should be? Are your GMAT results not what you wanted them to be? Do other problems exist that you feel will be a detriment to your being accepted? These issues and more will be addressed in this chapter as we examine the various criteria that will be considered as your application file is evaluated. This chapter describes the usual standards applied and the ways you can address the problems that might arise along the way.

At this juncture, we need to review some key points:

- There is a program that is right for you and that will accept you.

- You should not make decisions for admissions committees by presuming that certain programs will not accept you; making that decision is their prerogative and should be left to them. If you have a keen interest in particular programs, then you have an obligation to yourself to seek acceptance into those programs.

- You must be honest with yourself and the committee because only in so doing can you prepare the most impressive and positive application and enhance your chances for acceptance.

A new idea to add to our list is that there are very few problems or issues that do not have some chance of being overcome. Some admittedly may take more time and effort than others, but they nevertheless have the possibility of being successfully addressed. The potential for success comes down to how much you believe in yourself and how committed you are to getting into that graduate business program that is right for you.

Undergraduate Grades

Your undergraduate grades have three characteristics with respect to the admissions process: They are one of the initial considerations; they are only one of the many considerations; and they cannot be changed. We will start out by examining the general characteristics that the admissions committees will look for.

Generally, an overall grade-point average of 3.2 or better will cause an initially positive reaction in the minds of the committee members throughout the most selective schools. This average applies to all majors but may be decreased to 3.0 for the majority of programs and may fall to 2.8 for majors that are more technical, scientific, pre-med, or viewed as being particularly demanding. Another factor that may be considered is the perceived quality of the university that awarded your degree, a consideration that, for justifiable reasons, will not be acknowledged but that may act in your favor. This subjective consideration will only be used, however, if your academic performance was very strong. Remember that one of the features sought is uniqueness, and your undergraduate school may be one from which they receive few applications. Regardless, your overall grade point is only the first step in the evaluation of your academic performance.

It may well be that your grade point was somewhat reduced by a disastrous semester or, even worse, by two or three such semesters. Taking required courses in which you had neither an interest nor an aptitude, adjusting to the trials and tribulations of being on your own, or having that infamous "roommate from hell" could have contributed to a lackluster performance.

Because such scenarios are commonplace, the committee will likely make a secondary evaluation based upon your performance during your last two years. The presumption here is that by that point you should have completed the transition to college life, you should have been in your major courses, you should have developed an interest in and an aptitude for those courses, and you should have made a commitment to performing to the best of your ability in those courses. An upward-sloping average or, preferably, a consistently strong academic performance in the last two years will receive favorable attention. One bad semester will be viewed as not being truly representative of your inherent ability.

Almost every application will encourage applicants to submit an additional, optional essay addressing any issue or issues of their choice. Should you decide to address a period of poor grades in your academic history, then do so straightforwardly and honestly. State the issue, describe the circumstances surrounding the issue, and if you believe that your academic record is not reflective of your ability to perform at the graduate level, state this and provide evidence that supports your position. Do not be overly apologetic. Address the important points head-on. If you stayed in your initial major too long before transferring to your final program of study, say so and stress your performance once you made the transfer. If your performance was hindered by the fact that you were overly committed to outside activities, say so. Provide a documented record of your accomplishments to substantiate the great demands made upon your time, impeding your leadership potential. Did you party too much, goof off too much, or not appreciate the opportunity being offered to you? Then admit to it and explain what you have learned and how your perspective has since changed. If you suffered a personal or family tragedy, you may want to state the circumstances and their impact on your ability to perform.

If there are schools that you have a strong desire to attend but you believe are unattainable because of your grades, then perhaps you should delay your application to those schools. Gain acceptance into an alternative program on a part-time basis only, for the purpose of establishing a new academic record, perform to the utmost of your ability in that program, and then apply to the programs of your choice. You can effectively use alternative universities to reestablish, improve, and document your quantitative skills. You can demonstrate your ability to perform at the graduate level, your commitment to succeed at that level, and your increased respect for and appreciation of the educational process. Finally, you can test how committed you are to pursuing the graduate degree.

The importance of your grades diminishes with the passage of time. If you have gained valuable life experience that has exposed you to a wide range of business activities and policies, received rapid promotions, or participated in some unique and strategic business decisions or projects, then be sure to bring these accomplishments to the attention of the committee. Such accomplishments will show that you are mature enough and motivated enough to undertake graduate study despite any past errors of judgment or indiscretions shown on your record. More will be said about the issue of work or other experience in a subsequent section of this chapter. For now it is sufficient to note that your undergraduate grades become less relevant with the passage of time and that your work and other experiences start to play larger roles in the admissions committee's evaluation.

The last phase of the review of your academic record will likely entail the review of specific courses. If the program to which you are applying is highly quantitative, then attention will likely be focused on the number and/or types of courses in mathematics, statistics, and economics you have taken and on your performance in those courses. Because of its importance in an MBA program, your ability to communicate will also be examined—your performance in English, speech, theater, and other courses that contribute to the development and enhancement of written and oral communication skills will be evaluated. The last aspect to be considered will be the breadth of the course work you completed—how has it contributed to your being an educated, unique, interesting person? A pattern of courses in a unique area, such as music, foreign language, or theater, when your major field was more technical, such as chemistry, engineering, or business, will generate a favorable reaction.

In summary, the committee will start by reviewing your overall academic record, but will consider many issues beyond your overall grade point. The main question the committee will be addressing at this point is whether you have the ability to complete the program successfully and possibly at an impressive level of accomplishment. Also underlying the evaluation will be an earnest attempt to determine whether you are that unique, interesting individual likely to succeed and positively reflect on the program. Your undergraduate record is usually the first but is far from being the only matter considered.

The GMAT

Your academic record provides one clue to your ability to complete graduate study; another clue is provided by your performance on the

GMAT. The GMAT is a second standard by which a diverse applicant pool is evaluated. It is viewed as a measure of potential program performance, particularly in the first year. (Two other chapters are devoted exclusively to describing this examination and to developing strategies for maximizing your exam performance. This chapter focuses only on the role of the exam in the evaluation process.) The GMAT attempts to measure your reading comprehension, quantitative aptitude and reasoning, verbal aptitude, and analytical writing ability. It makes no attempt to measure your knowledge of business nor is it a predictor of long-term success in the business world.

A perfect score on the GMAT is 800 points. A perfect grade point is considered to be a 4.0. At one time it was common practice to multiply the grade point by 200, causing an academic record to be equally weighted in total points (200 × 4.0 = 800) with the GMAT score. If your grade point was a 3.4 and your score on the GMAT was a 520, multiplying your grade point by 200 would produce 680, which when added to your GMAT, would result in a total score of 1,200. This score would then be compared against a standard established by the institution. If your 1,200 exceeded that standard, then you would be a prime candidate for an automatic admit. If your score fell below another standard, such as 1,100, then you would be a prime candidate for rejection. Any score between the top and the bottom usually led to committee review. This practice of generating "magical" admissions formulas is less prevalent today but nevertheless continues to be employed by some programs. For many more programs, however, a more apt description of the role of the GMAT score is that it is an additional bit of information that is considered along with other characteristics in evaluation of your potential.

There is another way of viewing the role of the GMAT. In the formula approach just described, a higher GMAT score can partially offset a lower grade point. Conversely, a higher grade point can partially offset a lower GMAT score. For example, if your grade point was 2.8, then an impressive GMAT score of 640 would equal the 1,200 total points exemplified earlier. A grade point of 3.5 combined with a score of 500 would also produce a total of 1,200 points. Of course, in instances of either the GMAT or grade point being much lower than would be expected given your high performance on the other measure, the committee will have questions about the reasons for the disparity.

Although it seems obvious that having a very high GMAT score is better than having a low score, there is no score that guarantees admission. A recent applicant who had a 720 GMAT, a strong academic record from a highly prestigious university, four years of entrepreneurial work experience, strong interpersonal skills, a dynamic personality, and strong long-term potential was not accepted by any of the schools to which he applied. On reviewing copies of his application, the reasons for this were obvious—he completely failed to convey his many outstanding attributes in his essays to the admissions committee.

The basic reference GMAT score is 600. Any score above this number will attract attention and will likely cause you to be placed on the mailing lists of many schools. A score in the range of 550 to 599 will be an acceptable demonstration of potential for many programs and will likely lead to close scrutiny of your academic record and other personal accomplishments and characteristics. A 500 to 549 score will raise serious questions, but does not mean automatic elimination from further consideration. It will, however, lead to very close scrutiny of your academic record. Under 500 means that those participating in the decision process will have to look for other evidence of your ability to successfully compete in the classroom. If your scores were not reasonably balanced between the verbal and the quantitative sections, then the committee will look for other evidence in your academic record with respect to that problem area. Some programs will consider one section more important than the other, and evaluate your performance with this in mind. If the program is highly quantitative, then the quantitative score will receive greater emphasis. If the program is more qualitative and case analysis based, then the reading comprehension and verbal sections will play the more important roles. Regardless of their educational focus, all MBA programs will require you to demonstrate a basic level of quantitative preparation, but most programs are a blend of both and will prefer a balance between the two sections.

The issue that now needs to be addressed is what to do if your score is not at the level that you know it should be at or that you feel is representative of your potential. One strategy is to stress that your performance in particular courses is a much more accurate reflection of your true ability than is your GMAT score. For example, if you did not do well on the quantitative portion of the GMAT but did do well in undergraduate math courses, ask an undergraduate math professor to write one of your letters of recommendation to emphasize your math ability.

Another but less desirable strategy is to directly address your performance on the GMAT. If there were reasons for your less-than-desired performance, such as your not feeling well on the day you took the exam, then there had better be something in your academic record to substantiate that your GMAT performance was an anomaly. This argument generally evokes a response—rarely shared with you—of, "If that's the case, then retake the GMAT, prove your ability, and get back to us." If you historically have not done well on standardized tests, you can address this too, but you will need to back up your claim forcefully—for instance, by showing that despite low SAT or ACT scores, you had a strong undergraduate record. If you can show that your scores were low but your record was consistently strong, then your position will become more tenable and you may stay in the running.

A third strategy is to retake the GMAT, in which case you'll benefit from evaluating why your performance was less than you know it should have been. If it just happened to be a bad day for you, perhaps simply retaking the GMAT is the answer. On the other hand, maybe you need help improving your test-taking strategies. If you have a test-taking problem, simply retaking the exam will not help. Chapters 9 and 10 contain suggestions for improved test taking and focus on the GMAT in greater detail. For now, the focus is on what happens if you retake the test.

The ways in which the results of a retaken GMAT are handled will likely be as varied as the programs to which you are applying. A few schools will look only at your first-time results. Others will average the results. Some will look only at your best performance and others will break down your performance by test section and only look at your best scores in each section. Yet another approach is to compare your latest score with your earlier performance and then make some subjective adjustment for your having retaken the exam. The presumption may be made that the first forty to fifty points of any increase in your score is the result of having taken a coaching course, regardless of whether you actually did take a course. Therefore, if you did not take a coaching course and your score markedly improved, then you should consider mentioning this in your correspondence to the program. At the very least, it cannot hurt your prospects.

Before you select a strategy, you need to be aware that you have every right to ask an admissions representative of any program what the policy is with respect to retaking the GMAT. You can expect and will receive an honest response. Knowing this will enable you to develop the best strategy for you.

Letters of Recommendation

Letters of recommendation are a very critical part of your application and must be given the appropriate level of respect. In truly borderline cases, they can be the deciding factor. Accordingly, you must begin with the very careful selection of those who are going to write those letters.

Note that the term *letters* has been carefully and consistently used and with good reason. Many application packets contain a form that your recommender can quickly and easily complete. Be advised that the best strategy may be to ask each recommender to submit a letter in addition to completing the school's form. A well-thought-out letter written to the director and containing specific comments about your personal characteristics, accomplishments, and potential for success in management is important to your application and will substantially add to the significance of the rankings checked on the recommendation form. The fact that time was taken to write such a letter conveys the sense that the author knew you on an above-average basis and that the strength of that knowledge and belief in you was such that you were worth more than just the minimal amount of effort. In addition, your recommender can make explanatory and/or expansive comments to strengthen the credibility of the recommendation.

These letters represent another opportunity to address your unique characteristics. When you ask people to recommend you, provide them with any relevant forms, ask them specifically to include letters in addition to completing the forms, ask when they plan to have your recommendations completed, and thank them at that time for their commitment to recommend you. Also provide them with copies of your resume and inform them of any pertinent issues, such as a GMAT score of concern, that you feel need to be addressed. If the recommendation process calls for your including the letters in a single packet, then contact your recommenders one or two days before the agreed-upon date to confirm the material will be ready at the agreed-upon time. You should also decide how you will obtain the material from your recommenders. If you are to pick up the material in person, a time and place should be arranged. If the material is to be mailed to you, you will be able to estimate approximately when it should arrive. Allow two or three days to elapse beyond that expected day and call if it has not arrived to confirm when, or if, it was sent. If the letter was to be sent directly to the institution, call two or three days after the agreed-upon date to confirm that it was sent. Once you or the school has received the material, be sure to again thank the recommenders. Either call or write a personal thank you. Allow a minimum of two weeks to a month to get all recommendation materials prepared and completed.

Consider now the issue of whose recommendation to seek. Name-dropping is out. Recommendations must say something about you to be effective. Recommendations only have value if they are written by someone who knows you well and can evaluate you in a work or volunteer capacity. You should not ask for a letter from a senator, a member of congress, or other political figure unless he or she really knows you. The use of a close family friend or neighbor, even if that person is a community or business leader, is not recommended if his or her comments will be brief and cursory. A neighbor or family friend who has had a long-time relationship with you and is a high-level executive is acceptable. Directors of nonprofit agencies for whom you have volunteered are another source to consider. Having a "good word" placed by a highly respected student currently enrolled or recent graduate is also an acceptable strategy. A letter from a prominent business executive, big donor, or alumnus can have a negative impact if the referral source only casually knows you, and it will be easy for an experienced reader to tell.

If you have work experience, then your supervisor should be the first person you ask. If you have recently changed supervisors, then either your previous one or someone with whom you have worked on a major or strategic issue should receive top consideration. If you might jeopardize your employment status by telling your employer about your intention to begin full-time graduate study, then it might be wise to forego this recommendation source. If this is the case, mention your concern in either a cover letter or the optional section of the essays. If you can't ask your employer, consider asking a peer with whom you have worked closely on a major project or who is highly familiar with your ability and the quality of your work. If, despite the various options available, you do not want to make your intentions known in your work environment, then your prior employment setting can be an equally fertile source of recommendations.

If you are able to obtain one or two recommendations from your work environment, then obtain your third letter, if needed, from the university from which you earned your last degree (assuming your degree was earned less than five years ago). If there is someone in the field you have selected for your area of concentration or specialization who knows your capabilities, then this person should be your first choice. If there is an area of the GMAT in which you had problems, and if you had a professor who can attest to your true skills in that area, then approach that professor for a recommendation. Alternatively, if there is a faculty member who knows you and who is an alumnus of an MBA program to which you are applying, you should seriously consider asking that person for a recommendation. Yet another strategy is to seek recommendations from one professor in a communications area and another in a quantitative area in order to substantiate your abilities in both areas.

Leadership skills are another important area of consideration. Is there a faculty member or a high-level manager who can attest to your leadership accomplishments and abilities? Only ask people who have seen you in active, strong, influential leadership roles. Peer colleagues should be viewed as a last resort or as tertiary references at best, and then only if there is some substantive, unique context in which they saw you in action.

Most programs will ask for two recommendations and some will ask for three. If only two are requested but there is a third person you feel can also contribute significant insights about you, then submit a third recommendation. Do not send more than four recommendations, and only send a third and fourth if they have something substantive and unique to contribute. Otherwise, submitting more than three letters starts to quickly interject negative reactions into the evaluation process.

Interviews

Interviews are an integral part of the admissions process at many universities. Some institutions now require them, even for international applicants, except under the most exceptional circumstances. Most prefer that you arrange an interview even when there is no requirement to have one. Regardless of whether you view yourself as falling into the marginal category, if you have the ability to thoroughly and professionally sell yourself and if you are really committed to gaining admittance to a particular program, then you should make every effort to visit the campus and to schedule an interview. This shows initiative, gives you an early connection and exposure to the school, and may also provide a competitive edge in the financial aid process. Should you live a great distance from a targeted school (as is the case with most international applicants), a telephone interview offers some of the benefits of a face-to-face interview.

You can gain as much from the experience of an interview as the institution can. Use the on-campus interview opportunity to evaluate the program and the campus environment. Visit at least one or two classes, preferably one in the quantitative area and one in the case analysis or qualitative area or one in your area of interest. Take the initiative to talk with students about their perceptions of the program content and quality. Inquire about program support such as placement, library facilities, computer accessibility and support, mentor programs, quality of faculty and access to them, and class size. Try to determine the relationship among the students. Do they cooperate and help one another or is it every person for himself or herself? Ask them what characteristics they feel they possess that led to their admission. Do not be surprised at the candid responses you are likely to receive. Try to interview students before your scheduled interview, as doing so will immeasurably enhance your chances of performing in a truly professional fashion in your interview.

The schools, too, will benefit from your interview. If you are as good as you think you are and can sell yourself as strongly as you think you can, those involved in the admission decision will become convinced that the right decision is to offer you one of the seats in the program. They will be better able to evaluate your potential to interact and to contribute to the program. They also will get a sense of how employable you are likely to be when you complete the program. The way you conduct yourself in an application interview combined with the information gathered through the application process will weigh heavily in admissions deliberations.

From a very practical standpoint, the interview enables you to meet a member of the admissions staff and possibly other members of the admissions committee. Some schools use students, alumni, or consultants in the interview process.

Regardless of the interviewing format, take advantage of it to convey your professionalism and other characteristics, leaving no doubt that you are one who should be—rather, must be—admitted to the program. You must approach the interview as you do any interview for a job or promotion. That is, thoroughly read and reread the school's literature. Determine what characteristics capture the culture of the program. Know the strengths of the program and the faculty. Be prepared to ask questions about those areas of interest to you. Be sure to inquire about any changes in the program or in the course offerings that might be being contemplated, about the rationale underlying those changes, and about the impact such changes might have on your program of study. Feel free to comment on how these changes would be important to your plans and objectives for your future. Ask some of the same questions you asked the students. Compare the responses for consistency. Should you find any inconsistencies, it is up to you to resolve them through further inquiry and observation.

Be prepared to participate actively in and contribute to the discussion. Be mentally prepared to present yourself in a totally professional manner. Try to determine if there are any concerns about you that you can address with further explanation or clarification. Realize that you will be under constant scrutiny and evaluation and that your interview can be the "point of sale." It is your objective to make that sale. Dress as a professional; act as a professional; prepare yourself as a professional; and be a professional. Because of the interview's importance, additional and specific information is provided in Chapter 11.

Experience—More than Just Work

When thinking about experience in the context of the MBA, it is common to think of work experience as the only relevant issue. It is important, however, to recognize that experience is viewed in a much broader context in the admission evaluation process. It is life experience that is being evaluated, which means that work experience is only a limited part of the concept. Other important experiences in your life can be equally impressive in the evaluation context.

Experience may be viewed as a screen for maturity. You probably have been away from the educational process for a period of time and have lived on your own. You have shed the cloak of protection provided by your parents or guardians and have had to make it on your own—providing for your own food, clothing, shelter; making income allocation decisions; encountering the realities of the world. You have also learned about yourself, including what you do or do not want to do in your life. How effectively you have utilized your time will be subjectively evaluated. Because you have been away from the educational process, the presumption is that you view that process from a more positive, appreciative perspective. You have chosen to return for the MBA because you are able to see how it can benefit you in attaining your life goals. With this enlightened personal perspective, the likelihood is that you will be an active, committed, responsible, serious, and interesting class member—in short, the ideal class member for any professor who is dedicated to the educational process.

Work Experience

During the early 1980s the relevance of work experience to the MBA went through a transformation. In earlier eras, having an MBA was the most important qualification employers looked for in applicants. Rapid increases in the number of MBAs awarded and the salaries demanded, regardless of prior work experience, however, caused American industry to evaluate the return on its investment in MBAs. Profit erosion caused by the inroads made by foreign competition exacerbated the problem. Workforce retrenchment by Fortune 500 firms became the pattern of the day, leaving the smaller, midsized, and venture firms to take up the slack. These firms lacked the ability to employ in a learn-on-the-job context and had to find people who could quickly step in and become productive employees. Those who knew the language and process of business were those who most clearly fit their needs. The market for the high-potential candidate with a promising future but without prior experience evaporated.

As one would expect, this change in the employment picture quickly began to influence admission criteria. Those involved in the MBA process also came to some other conclusions. One was the belief that students who came straight from undergraduate programs knew that they wanted the MBA but frequently had limited visions of how to utilize such programs to their best advantage. A second was that when students without experience were intermingled with students with experience, the inexperienced students felt intimidated and became less active in the classroom, sometimes to the point of passivity. A third was that the inexperienced undergraduate did not fully appreciate the virtually unlimited opportunities of graduate study, but instead viewed the graduate degree as a continuation of undergraduate study. That is, they viewed the MBA as a necessity rather than a new, invigorating educational adventure. The end result was that it became and continues to be much more difficult for an undergraduate to enter into an MBA program without work experience.

What If You Don't Have Work Experience?

Should you abandon all thoughts of applying for admission directly from an undergraduate program? The answer is a qualified "no." If your other credentials are in near-perfect order—if you have a near-perfect academic record, a strong GMAT score, an ability to demonstrate an unusually high level of maturity, a well-above-average record of extracurricular accomplishments and leadership, a sound rationale for earning the MBA now rather than later, and strong ideas about why there will be minimal problems in placing you upon completion of the program—then you have a chance of being selected. The reason is that nearly every program will admit at least a few individuals who have little or no full-time, professional work experience. A review of their credentials, however, invariably displays an exceptionally high level of accomplishment and personal development that tends to be unique and well above that of their peers. Included in this context are summer internships, entrepreneurial initiatives, and co-op experiences, all having the potential to equate to the full-time experience customarily sought. Request an interview and be prepared to highlight your leadership in campus organizations, to relate your leadership experiences to management, to convey what you can contribute to the program, and to explain why you want to earn the MBA without first gaining work experience.

What If You Have Work Experience?

What issues are important and should be stressed if you have work experience? One of the keys is to demonstrate how earning the MBA will help you accomplish your personal and professional goals. What specific factors are considered? One will be your progression path. That is, were you assigned increasing levels of responsibility? In this context, titles assigned play less of a role than do the responsibilities assigned. How varied were your assignments? Having stayed at the same responsibility level while being introduced to a wide range of experiences will weigh heavily in your favor. Were you on a single, extended strategic project that enabled you to achieve a level of expertise and to influence the direction of a business unit? Focus on the challenges you faced, your contributions to and accomplishments within your organization, and the value you added to the project or organization. Weave the characteristics of what you learned and experienced into how the MBA will enable you to move to the next higher level, and you will have an essay that will impress those making the decision about your acceptance.

What If Your Experience Is Not "Conventionally Corporate"?

What if your experience was not that of the conventional corporate applicant? What if you opted to join the Peace Corps or you pursued a professional career in music, the theater, art, or a sport? What if you served in the armed forces, as an officer or otherwise? If experiences enhanced your credentials, helped to clarify your life objectives, contributed to your attaining a higher level of maturity, then incorporate them into your essays. Diversity in the makeup of the class is a highly desired objective, in which case your unique experiences should work to your advantage. Your objective now becomes one of showing how your experiences have influenced your life, relate to your decision to study management, and brought about your decision to pursue the MBA, as well as how the degree will contribute to your long-term goals.

What If You Have Job-Hopped?

A history of frequent job changes raises red flags in the minds of committee members. Interpersonal skills, commitment, ability to focus and to stay on track, all key to MBA program success, become open to question. The issue here is not your ability but your employability. If your resume documents a history of frequent changes in employers after short periods of time, such as every six months, then the committee will want to know why. One justifiable argument could be that you are energetic and are constantly seeking new challenges and rapid increases in responsibility. Another might be that you are one of those people who make strong, immediate, positive impressions on others so that new opportunities are constantly being presented to you. Or it may be that you have a personal problem that needs to be addressed before you pursue the MBA and start your career path anew. It is up to you to discern whether a problem exists and, if so, to decide how that problem needs to be addressed.

Extracurricular Activities

Remember how important extracurricular activities were in your applications at the undergraduate level? They are equally important in the graduate application process. The number and the types of activities are considered, but it is the substance of your contributions, the display of leadership roles, and the development of your leadership skills that will play the greater roles in the evaluation process. If you held positions of leadership, be certain to make them known to the committee and to stress the roles played and substantive contributions made in that context. It remains true that of two applicants with the same relative employment history and work-related experiences the one with a record of volunteer or other outside activities will receive the stronger positive reaction in the evaluation process. A record of substantive participation will be a plus, and a record of leadership accomplishments will be an even bigger plus. This will not be an overriding consideration, but should you have that record, neither overlook nor downplay it. Do not, however, inflate your record with activities in which you played an insignificant role.

Leadership Skills

A common theme here has been the importance of leadership skills. There are numerous ways to exhibit your talents in this area, the most obvious being through listing titles you have held. Another is through outlining your promotion path. A third is through describing the initiatives in which you have taken the lead such as the starting of your own business, perhaps as an alternative to the more traditional forms of summer employment, while completing your undergraduate degree. Major accomplishments, such as establishing new sales records or overseeing improvements in business processes are also relevant.

Should you not have a demonstrable track record of leadership, then you should consider taking steps to establish one. Consider participating in a group that focuses on developing these skills such as a Dale Carnegie course or Toastmasters. Review the offerings of a local university. Check with your employer's human resources department to determine if any pertinent programs are being offered in-house. Consider becoming active in a volunteer capacity and then accept the leadership of committees or projects. You may want, for example, to consider getting involved with Habitat for Humanity, the reason being that this group continually initiates home-building projects that require people to take charge of the work teams and take responsibility for the completion of the project itself. Finally, is there anything in the program to which you are applying that would help build your leadership skills? If so, then use this to your advantage by acknowledging that you need to develop those skills and commit to doing so as part of your program plan.

A Remaining Issue—the Essays

One critical part of the evaluation process has not been addressed in this chapter—the essays. The next two chapters will tackle the essays, and then we will examine the GMAT.

7

The Essays—How to Present Yourself

Essays are an all-important component of the application process, and they have two major characteristics. First, they are the one factor in the process that can almost totally make or break your chances of admission. Second, they are the most difficult and time-consuming part of the process. You will probably spend between five and fifteen hours writing each essay. Do not be surprised, however, should you find the first set taking longer. Later ones will likely take less time.

Because of the significance of the role of the essays in the application process, it is imperative that you read in great detail and closely follow the suggestions made in this chapter, which gives step-by-step writing strategies, and the next, which provides a close look at specific essay questions and actual responses.

What Does the Committee Want to Hear?

Asking, "What does the committee want to hear?" while being the most frequently asked question, is absolutely and unequivocally the worst way to plan a writing strategy. Ask any admissions committee member about the most important characteristic in an essay, and he or she will respond, "Honesty." Why? Easy. Admissions committees, above all, want to know about you and your personality in order to get to know you. Much time and effort is spent designing essay topics that do everything possible to get you to show your personal side. Writing essays in an attempt to give the committee what it wants to hear is not an honest approach and will sound artificial and generic.

Every prospective MBA dreams of the magic essay that will get him or her in automatically. Unfortunately, there's no magic formula. Many admissions committee members will tell you that they don't know what they want, but they know it when they see it. There are, however, certain characteristics that must be present, one of the most important being value added.

Value Added—A Most Helpful Guideline

A concept that has immense potential to greatly enhance your efficiency and effectiveness in attacking the essays is that of *value added*, a phrase currently in vogue and borrowed from the business world. As you review each of your life experiences, a question to ask and carefully consider is, "What was the impact of that experience?" What did you gain from that experience? How was your life influenced or enriched by that experience? What value was added to your life? How did that experience change you as a person or as a manager? If you were a contributor to the experience, whether it was for a job, a student organization, or something else, what substantive contributions did you make to the situation? What value did your participation add? Your responses to the essays must effectively address what value was added to you, what value you added to the organization with your efforts, and what value you would bring to the program. Convey that value and you will have gone a long way toward convincing the admissions committee that one of the seats in the program should be reserved for you.

What You Must Convey About Yourself

First of all, think about the essays as an integral component of the application. Why are they there in the first place? Upon reading the catalogs of the various business schools in the country, you'll note that each school, virtually without exception, states that it seeks to admit interesting, motivated, mature, unique, intelligent, and career-minded individuals. This is the reason for having so many specific essays. In order to find such people, dozens of challenging and distinct essay questions are asked of applicants. Each essay requires an honest, thoughtful, and insightful answer. Honesty is a virtue in any essay just as it is in life. This quality, above all, must characterize each of your essays.

Your goal in writing the essays, of course, is to get into the program. If the admissions committee walks away from your essay thinking anything less than, "We must have this person in our program," your chances of being accepted have been significantly reduced. Thus, the problem becomes a marketing dilemma. Briefly, you must present a persuasive, forceful, logical, honest, unique, interesting, and insightful argument for your admission into the program. You must present yourself as a unique person with something attractive and fresh to add to the school and to the classroom. You must convey how you see yourself fitting in to the professional world. Most important, you must come across as motivated and mature, someone who knows why the MBA is the right choice at this particular time, someone whose past has led to this point, someone whose career plan requires an MBA.

Almost every admissions representative will say that his or her school seeks individuals who are clear and forceful in articulating why they wish to pursue the MBA and why the MBA is a necessary and strategic career move. You must have a good degree of focus about your future and be able to articulate that focus in your essays. Woven into the argument for why you must obtain your MBA will be your past experiences, both professional and educational. A committee member must be able to read your essays and think, "Yes, it definitely makes sense for this person to get the MBA at this time; I can certainly see how this decision has evolved and come to fruition based on this person's experiences. I think the career plans are sound and the study plans fit with those career plans." The undercurrent that must flow through each and every essay, no matter the topic, must address, "Why the MBA? Why now? How does it fit into my plans for the future?" Why are clear career plans so crucial to an admissions committee?

Remember that the stated goal of these programs is to train managers and business leaders. If you cannot present what is in essence a business plan for your career, your ability to submit a business report or plan in the professional arena must be questioned. Admissions committees expect you to take the same kind of care with your application presentation and content as you would with a report or plan you submitted in a management position. So start now to think through why you are seeking an MBA and begin to formulate a business plan for your career—a career that necessitates the MBA. Again, you must be honest, thoughtful, and insightful.

Don't, however, mistake this advice to mean that applicants who succeed in gaining admission are only those who have very precise ideas about what they want to do with the rest of their lives. In fact, many prospective MBAs are in periods of transition in their lives. You may be reevaluating your career, hoping to change directions, but unsure exactly which direction to take. If that's the case, be honest. Say so! Changing careers is actually a good reason for pursuing an MBA. The point is, it is much better to be honest than to be falsely precise about your future. On the other hand, vagueness is not a virtue, and most successful applicants write essays revealing a strong sense of purpose. If you cannot make a convincing argument for beginning an MBA program to yourself, then perhaps you should seriously consider not doing so at this stage in your life.

How to Say It

The medium in which you must convey all of these qualities is writing, and you must take care to write extremely well. There's no question that writing style makes a difference. How you communicate is important—you must be able to articulate your thoughts in a clear and concise fashion. Good writers are convincing and engaging. Their ideas flow smoothly, making the reader's job much easier and more enjoyable. Admissions committees tend to be sensitive to poor writing skills because they want their programs to be known as sources of literate future business leaders.

You must write your own essays in your own words. Having someone review your essays and suggest improvements is an intelligent and acceptable way to improve the quality of your essays. Having your essays edited and sanitized by a professional, however, may very well set off alarms for committee members, who will be able to tell if you have not submitted your own work. Committee members have a number of very effective ways of detecting such misrepresentation. For example, they can compare your GMAT verbal score to the quality of writing in your essays. Similarly, your scores on the Analytical Writing Assessment sections of the exam can be compared in the same way. Committee members can also compare the language skills you demonstrated in the essays with those demonstrated in your telephone conversations and interviews. Some committee members also compare the essays to other writing samples submitted by the applicant, such as cover letters and correspondence—which are almost always composed by the applicant himself or herself. Any major discrepancy in quality between your essays and any of these sources will quickly raise concern and cause a committee member to investigate further. The more numerous and distinct the differences, the greater the likelihood that the essays will be downgraded in terms of perceived quality and reliability, even to the point of causing your application to be discounted altogether. If your writing skills are in need of significant improvement, rather than hiring a professional writer or editor, seriously consider taking an English writing course prior to taking the GMAT and writing your essays, especially if you plan to attend and to perform well at a top business school.

To make the task of writing even more challenging, you must be specific in your approach and answers while also being interesting. This doesn't mean that you must know in which position and company you will work, but it does mean that you must use specifics to support your answers. You must be able to organize your thoughts because you'll be faced with length limitations. Further, you must take care that your essays look professionally prepared.

The Five Criteria of a Good Essay

Specifically, you must be sure that your essays have the following qualities:

- **Clarity of purpose** A sense of direction must prevail. Do you know why you wish to obtain your MBA? Have you thought through your career path? Do you know what you intend to get out of an MBA program, what skills you intend to develop in the process, and how you envision using your education in the future? Have you been specific in stating your purpose?

- **Clarity of expression** Have you carefully articulated your response? Have you avoided reiterating information contained in other parts of the application? Have you made your points concisely, supporting your assertions with specific facts about you, your background, and your personality? Are your essays well written, detailed, and responsive to the question? Have you neither overelaborated nor understated? Have you avoided a monotonous tone and style? Have you avoided using too many big words and ambiguous adjectives? Have you adhered to word limitations?

- **Uniqueness of expression** Have you presented yourself as an interesting individual? Have you shed new light on an old subject, given a fresh slant to a common notion? Have you used a "hook"—an angle that will set you apart from the rest of the crowd? Will an admissions officer remember you? Have you identified and stated the value of your life experiences and how they help define you as a unique person? Have you avoided writing a dry, overedited essay that will put the reader to sleep? Have you conveyed your personality effectively to the committee through your essay answers? Have you shown different facets of your personality, without being outrageous? Could a close friend read your essays and confirm that they depict you? Have you been entertaining without being gimmicky? Have you captivated your reader? Have you said what you feel? Have you been careful to back up wit and humor with meaningful points? Does your expressed uniqueness mesh with the rest of the application?

- **Forcefulness of expression** Have you presented a persuasive collection of essays that will successfully "sell" you to the committee? Have you marketed yourself as an invaluable addition to the program? Have you avoided being unduly modest? Have you properly "tooted your own horn" without sounding too arrogant? Have you been justifiably proud of your achievements? Have you said something? Have you forcefully conveyed the value that has been added to you, the value that has been added by you, and your willingness and ability to add value to the program?

- **Honesty of expression** Have you given the committee "you, the whole you, and nothing but you"? Have you been frank about your strengths and weaknesses? Does the reader get a real sense of your worldview and personality? Honest essays are the best essays

to read and the easiest to write. Concocting ridiculous anecdotes, attention-getting schemes, or a fictitious portrait is a big
waste of time and energy. You must be vibrant but not gimmicky.
You must be businesslike in your approach, but don't feed the
committee dull, pompous lines.

In summary, have you presented everything in an honest, focused,
concise, unique, interesting, thoughtful, forceful, compelling way? It
is imperative that each of your essays contain these qualities, which
we will consider in greater depth in the next chapter. At this point,
we will turn our attention to writing strategies.

Essay Writing Strategies

One of the hardest things for any writer to do is to begin putting ideas
down on paper. In the next few pages, we will discuss strategies for
getting started. If you have not written any autobiographical or personal statements about yourself since high school, this process can be
alien and frustrating. One of the most important things to remember
throughout the process is to relax. Have fun with the essays! If you
do, it will show in your responses, and the admissions officers reading your essays will pick up on your enthusiasm.

Writing Strategy 1: Start Early

Successful essays take much time, thought, and rewriting. Do not
wait to start until a month before the application is due because by
that time it will be too late. Pick a target completion date somewhere
around four months before the application deadline. Begin at least
three months in advance of this target date and plan to spend at least
thirty writing hours on your first application. Remember, you'll be
starting from scratch on the first application. Gather together all of
the applications for all of the schools to which you will be applying
and read the essay questions. Read them every day after that, so that
they will remain constantly in the back of your mind. Then you will
subconsciously begin to formulate general responses in your head. This

is the optimal situation to be in three months before the target completion date and will prime you for the next step.

Writing Strategy 2: Review Your Life, Experiences, and Goals

This is tougher to do than it sounds. It is very difficult to think about and remember experiences, accomplishments, and other relevant facts. You can make yourself more aware of your experiences and goals by brainstorming. This is an important preparatory strategy because it makes you think in specifics. The best way to brainstorm is to pick up paper and pen and begin to make lists, asking and answering some important questions about yourself.

A. Make a Few Lists

To get your memory working, make lists of all of the following:

- honors, awards, or distinctions
- extracurricular activities
- community and professional activities
- leadership positions
- hobbies and avocations
- all full-time, paid positions you've held
- accomplishments in those jobs
- publications, research papers, special projects, and so on
- significant personal events and achievements
- career goals
- things that make you happy

Take about three weeks to complete the lists. You will begin to remember more and more things as you go. Don't leave anything out. Your goal here is just to put down on paper as much as you can remember, no matter how unimportant or irrelevant you think it is.

B. Think, "What Kind of Person Am I?"

Write down simple adjectives to describe yourself—nothing complicated. Just get your ideas in writing. Be as specific as you can. Ask friends to help you. You might, for example, come up with descriptions such as *motivated*, *career-minded*, *competitive*, *analytical*, and *ambitious*. Pick the top five qualities that best define you.

C. Think, "What Evidence Shows That I'm This Type of Person?"

Now relate the lists you made in Section A to the adjectives you came up with in Section B: Which events or experiences in your life best show each of your qualities? You may even answer this question with a written paragraph. Your goal here is to substantiate your assertions about yourself. At the very least, match up on paper each of the five qualities that best describe you with two or three experiences or achievements.

D. Think, "What Do I Want to Do with My Life?"

Write short answers to all of the following questions:

- What kind of position do I want following business school?
- What about five years after graduation? Ten years?
- What kind of person would I like to be then?
- What is the relationship between the MBA and my career goals?
- How will the MBA help me attain my goals?
- What is my vision of myself in the future?

This will take some time, but it will be time well spent. The answers to these questions will form the heart of most of your essays and will provide you with an excellent self-analysis.

E. Think, "What Have I Done with My Life?"

Think about your past and where you've come from to reach this point in your life. Write short answers to all of the following questions:

- Why did I go to college?

- Why did I study what I did?

- How did I get my first job?

- Why did I pick the jobs I've accepted to this point?

- Have I changed my goals? My interests?

- What has led me to the pursuit of the MBA?

Thinking about your past is important because it gives you a view of the stages you've gone through and decisions you've made that have led you to determine that the MBA is right for you.

F. Link Your Past, Present, and Future

Now relate the answers in Section D to the answers in Section E. Note how the past has led you to where you are now.

Writing Strategy 3: Make an Outline

This is a mandatory step in most types of writing and is most critical for your admissions essays. With a good outline to follow, writing the essay itself is fairly easy because you will already have done the hard part: the thinking. Outlines are critical to ensuring that you are answering the questions asked. Outlines also ensure that all of your ideas are included and that they are presented in logical sequence, making your essay flow smoothly from idea to idea. An outline provides organization—a well-planned and well-developed introduction, body, and conclusion.

Write an outline for each different type of essay you face. If two essay questions are very similar, however, you needn't write two entirely different outlines. To determine how many outlines you need to write, gather all of the essay questions from the applications you intend to complete, thoroughly review the questions, and then group them. Doing this will not only help you determine those essays which are closely aligned, but will also give you a comprehensive view of all of the topics you will have to address.

When constructing your outlines, be sure to include the following:

- Introductory paragraph: the customary main idea or thesis statement and an attention-getter

- Body: answers to the explicit essay questions, supported with specific examples and details, and answers to any hidden, unwritten questions (described and exemplified in the next chapter)

- Conclusion: summary of your thoughts and, where appropriate, your response to the questions, "Why get an MBA?" and "Why now?"

Writing Strategy 4: Write a Rough Draft

You should count on writing at least three drafts of each essay. Anything drafted fewer than three times is still rough and not truly competitive. Successful applicants write and rewrite several times before being satisfied with a final draft. Start by getting a first draft on paper. Use your outline, adhere to word limits, and adjust your answers to address the particular school.

Constructing a great introduction is crucial. Remember that admissions officers read thousands of answers to the same essay topic. The introduction is a very influential part of the essay and one of the hardest to write. A powerful introduction will wake up the reader, and chances are then very good that the reader will read the rest of your essay with interest and attentiveness. A poor introduction tells the reader that she or he is about to read another one of thousands of similar, ho-hum essays. It is a good idea to write the introduction after you have nearly completed the body and perhaps even after you have completed both the body and the conclusion—in other words, last.

The body of the essay should directly address the question asked, focusing on the aspects of your life that specifically support your answer. The ideas must be developed fully. You must always remember to interpret the relevant parts of your life for the reader. What did you learn from a certain experience? What value can be found in the experience? How did it contribute to your desire to get an MBA?

The conclusion should flow logically from the body and, like the introduction, give the reader a favorable impression of you.

Remember, your essay should be personalized—that is, directed toward the particular topic and program—rather than seem "canned," and it should end on an upbeat note.

Adjusting the essay to the reader is an important aspect of writing an appropriate response. Remember that your reader will play a pivotal role in your acceptance or rejection. You can safely assume that your reader will be intelligent and eclectic in background. Be assertive without being cheeky and disrespectful. You can assume that your audience is sympathetic to you, but don't depend on that sympathy to get you an indulgent reading. Don't assume that your readers are so sympathetic that you need not persuade them of your excellence. If you ever find yourself thinking, "They'll know what I mean," you're in trouble. Clear, well-developed ideas gain reader sympathy.

Writing Strategy 5: Proofread, Edit, and Rewrite

If you scrimp on this step, all of your effort will be for naught. The essential ingredient of the successful essay is time—time to think and rethink, time to write and rewrite, time to read and reread, time to proofread and reproofread, time to edit and reedit. Never read and rewrite an essay on the same day. Give it time. When you return to your essays, you will see them in a fresh light.

There are two levels on which you must edit your essays: content and mechanics. First, read your essays for content. Are you satisfied with what you've said? Have you taken advantage of every opportunity to forcefully and honestly incorporate the value-added concept into your essays? Do they meet the five criteria of a good essay? Have you conveyed the image you wish to project? Should certain ideas be expanded? Should others be deleted? Make wise use of your red pen—be as objective as you can. Put yourself in the reader's place. Do you walk away saying, "Wow! We need this person in our classroom!"?

Second, check your mechanics. Check spelling, grammar, usage, and punctuation. Use a dictionary and thesaurus. Make sure that your essays are as mechanically tight as they can be.

Rewrite your essays, making corrections, additions, and deletions in content and mechanics. Let the essays sit on your desk for a week or so and then go back to them. Chances are that you will think of yet other changes you wish to make. Take care, however, not to edit out the "flavor" of your essays. This is a fine line to walk; overediting and underediting are both shortcomings to a successful essay. If you've followed these strategies and kept in mind the five criteria of a good essay, you'll have successful essays and a successful application in your hands.

Finally, don't forget how important it is to write your own essays. Do not hire another person to write your essays for you or to so thoroughly edit your essays that admissions committee members can tell that you played little or no role in creating them. Recall that your essays can be easily compared with other representations of your ability in written English—your GMAT verbal score, your Analytical Writing Assessment essays, and your correspondence. A glaring inconsistency can cause the rejection of an otherwise superior candidate.

Writing Strategy 6: Professionally Complete Your Application

Suggesting that you professionally complete your application probably strikes you as stating the obvious. After all, why would you put so much time and effort into the process only to diminish the quality of your efforts by submitting a sloppily completed package? With the universal availability of word processing materials and equipment there is no justification for submitting something representing a less than professional effort. The suggestion is made for two reasons, the first is to ensure that you use all available sources of help. The second is to introduce you to two options that are available.

One option is a software-based system called MBA MULTI-App, which contains the application material for over fifty well-known programs, including most of those on everybody's top twenty to top forty lists. Use of this source is based on a flat fee but with the option to download a trial copy of the software from MBA MULTI-App's Web site. Included in the software is a *Core Questions* section that contains those questions common to all applications of the participating schools and thus need to be answered only once. Essays and unique questions are provided in each school's *Specific Questions* section. One additional helpful feature enables you to copy and paste similar answers from one school's application to another. Once the application for a particular program is completed, the software produces an exact replication of that school's application material, with your information and responses included. MBA MULTI-App also contains a feature called FIRSTLOOK that uploads information about you to a Web site. Admissions staff members can then visit the site to learn about you. Also provided are recommendation forms and transcript request forms. Financial aid forms, however, because of their extensive differences, must be obtained from the specific programs. Also, you will still find it necessary to order a school's brochures and other informational literature or visit its Web site.

To obtain more information about MBA MULTI-App, or to order it, call 1-800-51-MBA-AP (1-800-516-2227) or fax 610-544-9897. The e-mail address is mcs@multi-app.com. Or you can write MBA MULTI-App, 740 South Chester Road, Suite F, Swarthmore, PA 19801.

A second professional source is College EDGE, which offers an on-line application service to more than forty schools. You will be charged no fee to use the system, but you will be charged the regular application fee of each school to which you apply. College EDGE provides the entire application form, including complete application instructions and the recommendation forms for each member program. The process begins with a Personal Profile which contains data common to each program. Input of your essays is, of course, a part of the system. Copy and paste features enable you to move information from one essay to another. All application material is spell checked and error checked. The application material cannot be submitted until the information for all fields required by the school is provided. Resumes can be incorporated, and transcript request forms can be downloaded to your printer.

There are several ways to communicate with College EDGE. Their Web site address is http://www.MBA.CollegeEdge.com. The address is 101 Townsend, Suite 333, San Francisco, CA 94107. Their phone number is 415-778-6262, and their fax number is 415-778-6263.

Do not worry that using either of these options will cause you problems. Each of the participating schools promises that it will neither favor nor discriminate against application material submitted through either of these sources.

A Final Reminder

As you approach the essays for your applications, keep the following hints in mind:

- Take your time, and take the essays seriously.

- Tailor your response to each essay and program; that is, personalize the essays.

- Be honest, focused, concise, interesting, unique, thoughtful, and forceful in your writing.

- Market yourself as a valuable addition to the school—persuade the admissions committee that the school needs you.

- Be aggressive in content and style. Make yourself stand out. Toot your horn—be proud of who you are and what you have achieved. Stress the value that has been added to your life. Stress the value that you have added or received through your experiences.

- Keep essays to the point and interesting.

- Prepare and submit a professional application package that impressively presents you.

People commonly make four mistakes in the application process. The first is not answering the essay question asked. The second is making grammatical errors. The third is using the name of one university in an essay required by another. The fourth is making spelling errors. The availability of spell-check features in word processing packages makes this last mistake inexcusable.

8

The Types of Essays and How to Address Them

There are approximately a dozen basic categories of essay questions that you could be faced with during the application process. Not every application has each type of question, but all applications will usually have at least three of the following types:

- You, the MBA, and Your Career

- Substantial Achievements or Accomplishments

- Leadership and Responsibility

- Self-Analysis

- Ability to Contribute in a Group Setting

- For Fun

- Ethical Dilemmas

- Painful, Difficult, Highly Challenging Experiences

- Creative Brainbenders

- Academics

- Class Diversity

- The Optional Essay

At present, the diversity and the group topics appear to be the "in" topics, while the painful experience, ethical dilemma, and creative brainbender topics may be on the wane. However, do not be surprised should they once again become popular. In the following pages, we will discuss each type of essay in detail and analyze some successful essays.

You, the MBA, and Your Career

This is perhaps the most important essay you will write. Every business school application has an essay that falls into this category, and most schools place it as the first essay to be written.

At the University of South Carolina, this is the only essay with the exception of essays required in the applications for two specific programs. Examples of the questions that fall into this category follow:

> Discuss your career progression to date. What prompted you to seek an MBA degree now? What type of job do you see yourself in immediately after receiving your MBA? What are your ultimate career aspirations? Describe your plans to achieve them. (Southern Methodist University)
>
> Describe your post-MBA short (+ 2 years out), medium (+ 5 years out), and long-term (+ 10 years out) professional goals. How do you see the Smeal College MBA degree assisting you in attaining these goals? (Pennsylvania State University)
>
> Explain how obtaining a Master's degree will assist you in furthering and achieving your primary personal and/or professional life goals. Why is now the best time for you to pursue a TEXAS degree? (This explanation should include, but not necessarily be limited to, a brief description of both your intermediate and longer-term career goals.) (University of Texas at Austin)
>
> a) In one or two sentences, please state your short-term and long-term career objective(s). b) How have your prior academic, personal, and professional experiences influenced your career plans? c) Specifically, how will MBA studies and your participation in the Georgetown MBA Program contribute to your career objectives? (Georgetown University)
>
> Please discuss your previous professional experiences, your long-term career goals and the role the MBA will play in those plans. What do you hope your contribution will be to an MBA environment? . . . (Duke University)

Ten years after graduating from the Michigan MBA program you are the subject of a magazine article. What would the article say about your professional achievements and career goals? In what magazine would the article appear and why? (University of Michigan)

These representative questions show why you must personalize each essay. The essay question used by Southern Methodist is presented first because it is the most encompassing. It includes nearly every aspect that might be covered in a question of this type—your career, the timing of your decision, and your ideas about your career after graduation. You are also required to discuss your long-term goals and your plans to achieve them. You should be sure to include information on how the MBA is going to fit into your career plan.

Next, refer to the question used by Pennsylvania State University. Most essays use the ambiguous descriptors of *short-*, *intermediate-*, and *long-term* to categorize goals. Penn State, in contrast, defines the specific time horizons to be used.

The essay questions of University of Texas and Georgetown are similar in that they request that you introduce your personal experiences into your response. Texas, in contrast to Southern Methodist and Penn State, requires you to evaluate not only your career goals, but your personal goals as well. Georgetown wants to know how your personal experiences have influenced your career plans.

Duke's question has been selected because it alone asks how you will contribute to its program. You will find that your potential program contribution is frequently the focus of a separate question in most applications.

The University of Michigan's question is the last one provided in this section. It was chosen because of its apparent uniqueness: It asks you to present your response in the context of an article. To do this, you have to respond as though you were an outside observer. Once you assume this perspective and reduce the question to its basics, you should find yourself describing the goals you have set for yourself, the plans you have for achieving them, and the way that earning the MBA will help you. Don't overlook the part that refers to the type of magazine. First, select a high-caliber magazine. Next, if you have indicated a preferred area of study in another part of your Michigan essays, then be sure that the magazine you choose reflects that career path.

Note that there are three attributes being examined at all times: who you are; what you want for yourself; and why the MBA is your choice. It is essential that you be clear about your purpose for getting an MBA at the particular school to which you are applying, clear on your career aspirations, and clear about what led you to decide to pursue the MBA. You must have a business plan for your career. Otherwise, you can't realistically know why you want to get your MBA, and you will be unable to convincingly articulate to the committee your need for an MBA. (Unfortunately, "in order to make more money" is an unacceptable answer although very probably an honest one. Fortunately, the objective of expanding your long-term career options is both honest and acceptable.) By fully and honestly answering this essay question, you will have prepared that plan. Notice how the following actual essay exemplifies the suggestions made for responding to this constantly asked essay question:

Response

The manner in which I envision my career developing is a direct result of the path that it has followed to date. Having provided myself with a solid quantitative foundation upon which to make business decisions, I decided that I needed to get better acquainted with the actual mechanics of business. Henceforth, after achieving my professional certification, I left the "nest," so to speak; I initiated a unique personal transition from a technical department into a consulting department. For the last year I have been in that department in a support capacity, which has exposed me to various business industries, functions and issues. These two different experiences have provided me with two similarly unique manners of viewing a business. I believe that I have seen "both sides of the fence." I have witnessed managers who are making decisions based strictly on the functional knowledge of their business, while simultaneously witnessing finance and accounting personnel who are crunching and interpreting the resulting numbers and making decisions based on their respective functional knowledge base, without a common link existing between the two. Unfortunately, I have also witnessed how the lack of one good general manager, who understands the entire business, can result in a preponderance of dysfunctional decision making which very easily can lead an otherwise viable company into financial ruin. Recently, I have been lucky enough to be part of several teams that have provided the necessary bridge to join the two functionally concentrated components of the same team. It is a tremendous feeling to witness employees and management, alike, as they begin to realize the total capabilities of their business, and simultaneously see it start to function effectively.

It is this type of experience, specifically, that I hope to build on following my completion of business school. During my time in this consulting capacity I have focused on providing reorganizational services to companies. This has allowed me to work with companies in various industries and geographical regions, all with one common trait—they are all distressed to some extent or another. It is this type of forum to which I plan to return—one of "crisis management" in which the emphasis is on result-oriented decision making. The very nature of many of a company's situations dictate that change be initiated and quickly. I find that this is an ideal environment in which to learn about "how a business operates." Due to the critical nature of the decisions being made, there are generally only short lag periods before the corresponding results can be witnessed. Thus, one is quickly able to view the entire cause/decision/effect loop and to learn from both successes and sometimes even failures. Also, as a member of a crisis management team, one generally assumes the role of one of the company's top-level executives; therefore enabling the crisis manager to gain general management experience at a much earlier point along his/her personal career path.

I envision this leg of my career lasting three to four years. I feel that by this juncture, I will have then gained the applicable knowledge and will have been exposed to an extremely wide range of business perspectives. At that point several possibilities can be visualized. One is that I will be at or close to being promoted to the top executive levels of my firm. A second is that I could be asked to assume the reins of responsibility for one of the firms that have been turned around. Regardless, I expect to be ready for major decision-making responsibilities in crisis management situations at that time.

In conjunction with my short- and long-term career goals, I believe that an MBA makes perfect sense for me at this point in my career. On the basis of my short-term objective to return to a general consulting environment, I feel that the tool set that I plan to develop while obtaining my MBA will allow me to function better, if not excel, within that type of an environment. Most of my current associates have recently returned from business school and the general business skill set that they possess affords them greater insight into the business problems that we are simultaneously tackling. Currently, the only means I have to learn this type of skill set is by observing and interacting with them on the job. In and of itself, this is an entirely acceptable means of learning; in fact I believe that it is a necessary means of gaining required experience. However, I believe that business school will provide a more effective forum for learning the concepts, techniques and mind-sets necessary for one to possess in today's complex business environment. Following the completion of business school, I plan to return to my current employer and apply my newly developed knowledge base against real world business issues. I believe that this line of progression will also position me strategically for several long-term options.

Outside of the aforementioned general reasons for "why I want an MBA," I also have some more specific plans of what I desire out of my MBA. As I mentioned previously, I am comfortable with my functional financial knowledge base. However, this is not to say that I would not benefit from brushing up on some accounting and adding to my finance education. These are both events that I do envision taking place. But the major impetus behind my desire to obtain an MBA is a need to better understand business as a whole. I want to see how the different functions of a business interact and affect each other and how the business as a whole interacts and affects its adjacent community. I plan to gain as much exposure to as many industries, functions, business problems and solutions as two years will afford.

Notwithstanding my desire to delve into the nuts and bolts of business, I also have an ulterior motive for wanting to attend business school. I have been actively involved in my respective community, irrespective of where that has been, for the better part of the last seven years. However, I still am not sure of where and how I want to focus my future efforts in this arena. I believe this is directly attributable to my lack of understanding of "what is out there in the world today." I feel that if I had to identify a weakness that I possess, it would be that I really am not as current on world and domestic affairs as I would like to be. I plan to use my business school experience to gain exposure to public opportunities, various cultures and differing mind-sets in order to broaden my horizons, in a sense. To help you better understand this motive, I see business school as a unique opportunity for me to grow and mature not only from a business standpoint, but also as a person.

Along that same line of thought, I see _____ as the ideal place for me to be able to both enhance my business knowledge and grow myself as a person. Based on my research, attendance at two information sessions, long talks with alumni, and even discussions with two of the admissions officers, I believe I have a good sense of the school's culture. I am intrigued by the [school's] commitment to the community and to the not-for-profit work which is very evident by the school's commitment to the not-for-profit program. I envision my own involvement in the community to continue to be ancillary to my professional demands; however I do plan to take full advantage of the opportunities to take not-for-profit courses while enrolled in your program.

. . . Overall, I feel that I have a unique business perspective and personality to add to the classroom discussions and to my classmates' growth processes, and I hope that I am given the chance to bring this to ____ because I am convinced that you will receive innumerable benefits in return.

Analysis

The essay is written in a generally straightforward and uncomplicated style, which is an acceptable style of writing. It is well written—the ideas are fully developed and presented in a logical progression. The body of the essay is strong, and specific experiences substantiate the assertions made. The conclusion is also strong because it shows that the applicant has thoroughly studied and evaluated the characteristics of the program. Overall, the essay does answer the three questions inherent in the essay question.

More is communicated in this essay, however, than answers to the direct questions asked. Some very important personal information is conveyed that makes this person a highly desirable candidate. Two examples of such information are the applicant's adventuresome or entrepreneurial spirit and high degree of self-confidence. This is indicated by the applicant's choosing to leave a very comfortable position for a less comfortable one in which a new and expanded range of job skills, perspectives, and knowledge would be required. The applicant also gives the strong impression of being highly respectful of those who have these expanded abilities and appears to be looking forward with enthusiasm to doing the work necessary to move to the next level of professional achievement. This applicant clearly responds well to and enjoys complex challenges and high-pressure situations. Finally, the applicant shows how the business program will contribute to his or her future professional development. On the basis of this essay, an admissions committee member would put the applicant into the "highly desirable" category and strongly lean toward admit, a decision that is, of course, subject to the strength of the remainder of the file.

Substantial Achievements and Accomplishments

This category of essay requires you to relate to the committee one to three situations or experiences that you view as personal or professional achievements or accomplishments. You can presume that you will get this question, or a very similar one, like Leadership and Responsibility, in one form or another on many applications. Representative examples of the questions in this category follow:

> Describe a significant leadership experience, decision-making challenge, or managerial accomplishment. How did this experience affect your professional/personal development? (University of Virginia)
>
> Discuss your most substantial accomplishment and what you learned from it. How will that experience contribute to your success as a manager? (University of Illinois at Urbana-Champaign)
>
> List one of your most significant professional or organizational accomplishments. Describe your precise role in this event and how it has helped shape you as a manager. (Emory University)
>
> What are the major accomplishments in your background of which you are most proud? How do they illustrate your ability to successfully pursue an MBA? (Ohio State University)

The importance of this essay is frequently underestimated by prospective MBAs. The answers you give to this type of question are very telling to an admissions committee member as they provide the committee with an excellent view of what gives you a sense of pride and achievement and what motivates you to achieve. You must carefully think through your answer to this essay.

The first step in answering this question must be deciding what to include as an accomplishment or achievement. Let's begin with a definition of *accomplishment* and *achievement*—the terms being synonymous for our purposes. A good definition for both terms is "an event or situation in which you successfully exerted a high degree of influence resulting in a sense of personal satisfaction that allowed you to learn something about yourself and, where applicable, contributed to your desire to get your MBA." So there are at least three and potentially four questions to ask yourself when selecting a topic:

- Did I influence the turn of events in some situation?

- Did this outcome give me a sense of personal pride, success, and satisfaction?

- Did I discover something about myself?

- Did this self-discovery influence my decision to get an MBA?

Ohio State specifically focuses on your pride and then requires you to relate that pride and experience to pursuit of the MBA. In contrast, University of Virginia, University of Illinois at Urbana-Champaign, and Emory University focus on what you learned from the experience and how that learning experience had an impact on your path toward personal and/or professional development. Implicit throughout, however, is the question of how these experiences influenced who you are and how they influenced your decision to earn the MBA.

As you can see, there are some unwritten and hidden aspects to this deceptive and multifaceted question. Few applicants are aware of the requirements of this essay. Far too much effort is spent by far too many applicants in trying to impress the admissions committee incorrectly.

The goal here is to impress the committee, though not with the achievement itself, but rather with why you were proud of accomplishing what you did. The magnitude of your achievements is not nearly as important as the self-awareness gained through the experience. Most applicants worry too much about impressing the committee with unbelievable or newsworthy accomplishments. Always remember that the committee members will not be rating or judging your stated accomplishments on an objective scale, nor will they objectively compare your achievements to those of other applicants. Your task here is to provide the committee with a close look at the growth and self-awareness you gained through your achievements. *Why* you consider a certain accomplishment to be substantial is all-important. There are no good or bad achievements, and no one's accomplishment is better than anyone else's. Refrain from asking yourself, "Is this achievement worthy enough for XYZ School?" Refrain from exaggeration—honesty is always impressive—yet be justifiably proud of your achievements.

Make sure that your discussion of any achievement (1) includes a straightforward and detailed description of the situation or event; (2) addresses why you consider it a significant achievement and why you derived a sense of pride and satisfaction from it; and (3) explains how this experience contributed to your desire and decision to pursue your MBA. The latter is not specifically asked but a good essay will touch on it. Remember, each essay must address at some level the question "Why the MBA?"

Finally, keep in mind that the achievements you choose to discuss should reveal your uniqueness and individuality. Try to steer clear of achievements that are universally common among prospective MBAs, as they will detract from your individuality. For example, because every applicant is a college graduate, it does nothing whatsoever for your case to list among your achievements your graduation from undergraduate school, no matter how prestigious or demanding the program. The desire to do so is easily understandable because each applicant feels that his or her particular undergraduate experience was unique. Admissions staff, however, tire of hearing about it. Should, however, your degree experience tie into another matter, such as your grade-point average, your being the first in the family to attend college and the unique related pressures that you thus faced, or the conditions under which you completed your undergraduate degree were unique (you worked sixty hours a week, completed an overload every semester, successfully presided over ten student organizations, and were able to complete the program in three years), then go ahead and work your earning of an undergraduate degree into your essay. Otherwise, you should carefully consider your use of this achievement. Use a bit of common sense, and you will be glad you opted not to be one of thousands claiming college degree completion as an achievement. Be a standout! Tell the committee members something they don't know about you. Consider the following example:

Response

At the beginning of my senior year, an economics professor asked me to serve as the tutor for his year-long introductory class. "There's one thing you should know before you commit to this job," he cautioned. "One of the new students is blind."

I admit that I was hesitant to accept such a responsibility. I knew that it would be a highly valuable and unique experience, but I didn't know how I would ever communicate economic theory without the use of visual aids. I was afraid that I lacked the patience necessary to succeed. Nonetheless, I hated to pass up the opportunity or disappoint the professor, so I consented. As with other students, "Jane" and I were able to discuss fundamental economic principles, but in order to convey the concepts graphically, I had to employ such tactics as drawing graphs on her hand and shaping her arms to represent supply and demand curves. Once she could conceptualize the figures, she learned to imprint the graphs on plastic sheets with a stylus.

Tutoring Jane was a challenge in many ways. At times, she tried my patience. At other times, I tried hers. When we first began working together, we planned to spend four hours a week reviewing the topics covered in class, preparing her homework assignments, and studying for exams. We quickly discovered that this was a gross underestimation of the time needed to accomplish our goals. Often, it would require an hour just to grasp a concept before actually proceeding to the assigned homework. By the end of our sessions, we were often just beginning to break new ground; to quit then would have made progress nearly impossible.

I found it particularly difficult to work on a problem when time was scarce. Though I knew I needed to pull the solution out of her Socratically, it was often tempting to simply give her the answer so that we could both go home. What made it more difficult was that she could easily sense a change in my tone of voice if I became frustrated. With our progress dependent upon the comfort between us, any frustration on my behalf could seriously impede the learning process.

One of the most challenging episodes Jane and I experienced was her first exam, for which I read the questions aloud and then wrote or drew her responses. That afternoon, my role changed from that of teacher to simply translator. At times this got to be quite upsetting, because she would devise an incorrect answer and, as much as I wanted to tell her that it was wrong, I had to construct the graph according to her directions.

I first realized that Jane had made notable progress when I held a group review session before the second exam. When one of the other students asked me to explain externalities, Jane spoke up without hesitation and described a graph and the theory supporting it. As the year went on, her understanding developed tremendously. Her confidence level markedly improved, as did mine. She began to take tests alone and grasped concepts more quickly. By the end of the course, she was a much stronger student than many of her classmates and even enrolled in intermediate microeconomics for the following August.

At the onset of the year, Jane was handicapped by my lack of experience in dealing with blindness. By May, however, we had both overpowered our limitations. I certainly cannot take all the credit for her success, because she is an extremely bright and determined individual. I do, however, take pride in my ability to accept a unique challenge and conquer an obstacle that I initially feared.

Analysis

There is no doubt that the importance of the applicant's accomplishment is forcefully conveyed. Of equal importance are the personal attributes that are conveyed. Humanism, professionalism, and empathy are evident throughout the essay. Frustration and the creativity needed to overcome that frustration are shown. The applicant addresses ethical challenges as well as the manner in which those challenges were addressed. There is also one important piece of information that could easily be overlooked, one found at the very beginning of the essay. Note that the professor sought out the author of the essay and not the reverse. This strongly and immediately suggests that this applicant had exhibited some very strong, highly desirable personal characteristics, characteristics that would be highly desirable in an MBA program. This sample essay should impress upon you that it is the personal information conveyed rather than the accomplishment that is critical.

Leadership and Responsibility

Leadership and *responsibility*, on the surface, appear to be synonymous with *achievements* and *accomplishments* but, as we shall see, there are some important differences. For now, consider the following representative Leadership and Responsibility essay question examples:

> In this essay, we would like you to address the following question: How would you characterize the effect of your contributions to the groups or organizations in which you have participated? We are interested in your perceptions of the personal impact you have made, rather than a listing of group achievements. You may, however, wish to cite specific examples to illustrate your meaning. (Yale University)
>
> Feel free to draw upon work experiences, extracurricular activities, or your personal interactions, describing a period of formal or informal leadership. Please focus less on the specific situation and more on what caused you to be effective. (Harvard)
>
> Discuss a situation, preferably work related, where you have taken a significant leadership role. How does this event demonstrate your managerial potential? (University of California—Los Angeles)
>
> Describe a situation in which you felt compelled to take a stand against the majority. How did the experience strengthen your understanding of leadership? (Indiana University)

This type of essay is included so that the committee can gauge your leadership and managerial potential. It is very similar to the Achievements and Accomplishments essay and, in fact, many applicants are unable to distinguish between the two.

There is a big difference, though, between an accomplishment and a leadership role. *Leadership*, for purposes of your business school application, means leading, managing, and being responsible for people. Examples include offices held, positions in the community, projects involving delegation of authority and responsibility, and group leadership in the workplace. Recall that we defined an *accomplishment* as a personal achievement—some challenge you met that resulted in personal success but that did not require leading a group of people. Think of it this way: All successful leadership positions are accomplishments, but not all accomplishments are leadership roles.

Refer, for example, to Yale's posing of the essay that makes a clear distinction between your personal impact (leadership role) and the achievement. Refer also to UCLA's essay, which focuses on leadership yet does not mention tying it to an accomplishment. The essay question used by Indiana University recognizes that simply taking a stand against the majority is in and of itself a difficult task that requires assuming a leadership position. Indiana does not ask what position you assumed or whether you were able to successfully defend your position; the focus is on what you learned from the experience. Harvard also focuses on what you learned but extends that focus to include determining why you were effective.

Recognizing the distinction between a personal achievement and a leadership and responsibility role will enable you to accurately and correctly respond to the question. This distinction is especially important on those applications that require both an Achievements and Accomplishments essay and a Leadership and Responsibility essay. You should never use the same experience(s) to answer completely different questions. Given that the major criterion defining and characterizing leadership and responsibility is managing people, your biggest task is to identify such a position in your experiences. Schools, remember, wish to train future business leaders, responsible people with great potential for success.

Like the Achievements and Accomplishment essay, this essay requires you to: (1) describe the leadership role or situation, (2) give an explanation of what you learned or affirmed about yourself and your management potential through assuming this responsibility, and (3) relate your self-discovery or reaffirmation to your desire to get your MBA. Again, as in the Achievements and Accomplishments essay and in all essays, this third point is usually the unstated question within the question. Look for it in the following essay:

Response

In the last seven years of my life I have been actively involved in my surrounding community, irrespective of where it has been. My involvement has ranged from helping underprivileged urban children to my recent election to cabinet status of the United Way. However, I believe the most inspiring volunteer work that I do is associated jointly with youths and sports.

I am a steadfast believer that athletes, at all levels, have an obligation to give back to their respective communities. In direct contrast to the comment of a well-known professional athlete that he was not a role model, I feel that athletes are role models to much of the United States' youth today. I know, that, as a youth, I personally idolized several professional personalities. Thus, I think that it is imperative that athletes today be very cognizant of the potential repercussions their actions, both on and off the field, can have on this generation of America's youth. Further, I feel that if at all possible, those fortunate enough to have played a game should make every effort to give something back to their respective sport. It is this mind-set that has prompted me to become involved with several youth programs in my adjacent community.

Recently, I was presented with the opportunity to coach a pee-wee football team, and admittedly I practically jumped at the chance. However, I could never have imagined the extreme satisfaction I would receive in helping these youths mature and learn both physically and mentally. The team's season lasted from late August through early November with practices being held three times a week and games on Sundays. I am thrilled to report that our team won the Midget League "Super Bowl" in a hard-fought victory.

The boys' ages ranged from nine to eleven, and this was the first time that most of them had ever played organized football. My job description as a coach was to teach the most basic of football fundamentals. However, I actually believe that I had a much greater obligation to these young men. I served as their role model, their disciplinarian, and most importantly their friend. Throughout the season, I believed that we reaped mutual benefits, as I provided them with basic football knowledge and they provided me with an emotional high. I can still recall driving home alone after practice and breaking into a smile or even all-out laughter recalling the events of that day's practice. The people in the cars driving in the opposite direction must have thought me crazy.

By the end of the season, several of the players had developed a habit of following me to my car after practice, reluctant to allow me to leave. We had developed a strong bond in a matter of just three months. Due to a drastic change in my work schedule, I was unfortunately not able to coach again this year. Nonetheless, I occasionally call several of my former players. I had the opportunity to go watch several of them play this year. Our championship season is an experience that I know I will never forget and one that I will always treasure.

I believe that the reason I find this type of activity so inspirational is that I really feel that it is possible to connect with the youth of today. I think sports are one medium that we can use to reach the next generation of our nation's leaders, and hopefully in some small way contribute to their individual growth processes.

Analysis

This essay could just as well have served as an example of a For Fun essay or of an Achievements and Accomplishments essay. It is put here to emphasize that the leadership positions and accomplishments cited do not have to be earthshaking in their impact to constitute an impressive essay. One senses that the applicant felt accomplishment and enjoyed the activity, feelings that would have existed regardless of the outcome of the season. A sense of humor, a sense of pride, and a willingness to contribute to society are also conveyed. One also gets the impression that the applicant viewed himself as an effective leader and so did the players. At first, a reader might tend to judge this essay as failing to demonstrate leadership ability because of the young age of the individuals being led. However, closer inspection supports the applicant's leadership ability at the adult level: Note that he was selected as a cabinet member of United Way. Presumably he would not have been selected if he had not shown a strong capacity for leadership. Also note that this point is made in the very first paragraph of the essay—it is not lost in the body of the text. The ability to convey these traits has helped place this individual high on the admit list.

Self-Analysis: Strengths, Weaknesses, and Some New Packaging

With the self-analysis essay, admissions committees are once again trying to get a sense of you as a person. Remember that lest you get lost in the three approaches that are taken to elicit this information from you. This essay, in its original form, is the familiar "discuss your strengths and weaknesses" essay (although the term *weakness* might not be used). As you will soon see, one form of repackaging this question incorporates it into a group context. Another form asks you to respond to essays that call for you to stress your strengths and avoid any discussion of your weaknesses.

It is best to be brief, honest, and pragmatic in your approach to this essay. Long-winded descriptions of numerous strengths and weaknesses are boring. Pick three or four of what you consider to be your outstanding personal strengths, along with a weakness or two (it's best to have more strengths than weaknesses), and concentrate on these. Careful thought will allow you to narrow your undoubtedly numerous strengths to a few significant ones. The problem for most applicants is in deciding what to include as a weakness or trait upon which they would like to improve. The real trick here, and what will make your essay a success, is to relate your weaknesses to your desire to get an MBA. It makes perfect sense to list weaknesses that can be overcome in the course of gaining your MBA at the school to which you are applying. Not only is this an honest and pragmatic solution, but it also reinforces the answer to the unwritten question running through all essays: "Why the MBA?" Of course you lack some sort of educational, theoretical, and/or analytical skill or ability. That is part of your reason for seeking an MBA. By elaborating on this aspect of your need to obtain your MBA, you simultaneously accomplish the goal of answering the question honestly and insightfully and advance your argument for admission.

Far too many prospective MBAs try the age-old tactic of couching actual strengths as weaknesses; this usually results in eye-rolling on the part of experienced admissions staff and committee members who are all too familiar with such ploys. Weaknesses such as "I'm much too thorough, too much of a perfectionist," "I have little patience for those less intelligent than I," "I work too hard," and "I'm an overachiever" usually get put into the "Give me a break!" file by the committee. Steer clear of this flawed and commonly used strategy or you will probably only damage an otherwise excellent application. By the same token, common sense dictates that you not list serious character flaws as weaknesses. You probably wouldn't want to describe your kleptomania, violent temper, or chronic lying to the admissions committee.

Finally, view this essay as yet another opportunity for you to distinguish yourself from the pack. Be sure to discuss the strengths and weaknesses you feel will make you a memorable candidate. Everyone has unique strengths and weaknesses, but not everyone is clever enough to discuss these qualities. Take this chance to make your reader react with, "That's different," rather than, "Oh, no! Not another . . ." Be sure to end on a positive note; discuss a strength last if you're writing a single essay covering both strengths and weaknesses or discuss how enthusiastically you look forward to improving yourself in the program. Each of the following essay questions requires self-analysis:

> Each of us has been influenced by the people, events, and situations in our lives. How have these influences shaped who you are today? (Our goal is to get a sense of who you are, rather than what you've done.) (Stanford University)
>
> Describe a mentor/teacher you admire and explain why you admire him or her. How have you incorporated into your life what you have learned from this person? (University of Alabama)
>
> Please provide us with a summary of your personal and family background. Include information about your parents and siblings, where you grew up, and perhaps a highlight or special memory of your youth. (University of California—Los Angeles)
>
> My family background is unique because . . . (Emory University)
>
> Be your own career counselor. What aspects of your personality or background present the greatest obstacle(s) to achieving your goals? (Southern Methodist University)

Stanford's statement, "Our goal is to get a sense of who you are, rather than what you've done," accurately and succinctly captures the substantive intent of this question. The four remaining questions have the same intent and differ simply in requiring you to respond under differing conditions. We'll examine a response that was submitted to one of these essay questions in a later section.

Ability to Contribute in a Group Setting

This essay question functions to keep the number of essays in the application down to a reasonable number by combining two distinct topics and to reflect the change in educational philosophy from stressing individualistic effort to embracing a group context. Hence, some essay questions in this category reflect this strange combination of attempting to discern your personal characteristics in a group setting while attempting to discern your strengths and weaknesses. Other essay questions are more straightforward and simply ask you to address only group issues. Consider the following examples:

> In this essay, we would like you to address the following question: How would you characterize the effect of your contributions to the groups or organizations in which you have participated? We are interested in your perceptions of the personal impact you have made, rather than a listing of group achievements. You may, however, wish to cite specific examples to illustrate your meaning. (Yale University)
>
> Tell us about the most challenging team experience you've had to date. What role did you play? What factors made it a challenge for you? How did you and the group address these issues? What did you learn? (Duke University)
>
> What is the most significant change or improvement you have made to any organization with which you have been or are currently affiliated? Describe the process that you went through to identify the need for the change or improvement to the organization, how you managed the process of implementing the change, and describe the results. (Georgetown University)
>
> Discuss your involvement in a community or extracurricular organization. How did you attain your position in the organization? How did you help the organization meet its goals? (Purdue University)
>
> What specifically have you done to help a group or organization change? (Harvard)
>
> Describe a group or team experience where you assumed a leadership role. Include how you handled any problems that may have arisen. (University of Illinois at Urbana-Champaign)

When developing your response to essays in this category, the first aspect to focus on is what the essay is seeking to determine—not what you *think* the essay is asking. For example, many applicants will address these essays by describing the group effort. Note that this is not the objective. First and foremost, you must remember that the major objective is for the committee to learn more about you—in this case, how you operate in a group or team context—not about what your group accomplished. The essay question used by Yale University summarizes the focus and the content that an impressive response should contain.

Note that both Duke and University of Illinois want a challenging or problematic group experience rather than a more conventional one. Both universities are asking the same question; Duke's specifications, however, do a better job of providing the guidance necessary for appropriately responding to the essay question. Georgetown's essay is very comprehensive in that it requires you to discuss change, the process for that change, your role in that process, (your leadership role in that experience), and what was accomplished. Purdue University is asking a very similar question but in a differing way. Purdue asks that the experience be outside of the workplace and in a voluntary capacity—in this way, it hopes to also discern how you use your leisure time. Purdue also assumes that you were selected to a position of leadership and wants to know why you think you were selected and concludes by requiring you to discuss what your leadership contributed to the accomplishment of the group. Harvard's essay question is more general in its content. Guidance for your response to this essay question can be found in any of the other essay questions cited. Your first objective is to determine the precise focus and content of the question at hand.

Once you have determined the focus and content of the question, the process becomes simpler. Select a group situation in which you played a major role. Determine three characteristics you exhibited in helping that group function and incorporate them into your response. Also determine some aspects about working in a group context that you found frustrating, such as getting all members of the group to carry their own weight or using your negotiating skills. At the end of your essay, mention these frustrations as skill areas you hope the program will help you improve.

Finally, note that with a slight change in emphasis these same questions could easily be transformed into leadership questions. Therefore, even though a leadership role may not be required, if you have played a leadership role on a successful group project, then by all means convey this fact whenever the situation permits.

For Fun

Example essay questions in this category follow:

In my leisure time I . . . (Washington University)

> Discuss your free-time activities and interests. What is your most rewarding personal activity? (University of Illinois at Urbana-Champaign)
> I have always wanted to . . . (Emory University)

While every school includes space in the application for listing hobbies and extracurricular activities, eliciting that type of information is not the objective of an essay of this type. Many applicants wonder why an academic admissions committee is even interested in what they do for fun. Be assured that this is indeed a very important essay and not one to be neglected or taken lightly. How you spend your free time is one of the best indicators of who you are as a person. Further, it tells the committee how well you will fit in with other students and how you will contribute to the social life of the school. The time you spend at business school can be a very social experience, and student-student interaction is quite important.

There are very definite strategies for answering this type of question. The immediate reaction of most applicants is to want to list dozens of activities: "I love to bike, swim, run, ski, golf, play tennis, play racquetball, hike, go to the theater, attend concerts, collect stamps, waterski. . . ." This unfocused approach misses the point of the essay completely. You will not get points for having the most extracurricular activities; it's not a contest. What you must realize is that this type of essay provides you with the ultimate opportunity to present yourself as a unique person. Capitalize on it!

First, pick one or two activities. Think of an empty, lazy Sunday. You have nothing but time on your hands. What would you most like to do with that time? That's the activity to discuss. Your discussion will be focused, enthusiastic, and enlightening without much effort. By discussing your favorite extracurricular activity, you will automatically be setting yourself apart from other applicants—most won't share your interest, and those who do will give different reasons for enjoying it.

Second, go into detail about your activity. Talk about the feeling you get when you participate and why you like it. Tell the committee why this activity is important to you—give a very personal view of you on your downtime. Don't fictionalize an activity just to impress the committee because your delivery won't be sufficiently sincere. Again, be honest! The activity itself takes second place to your detailed, personal feelings about it. Provide the reader with a powerful sense of the importance of the activity to you.

As you think about and begin to write about your leisure time, try to allow your reader to share in your interest, enthusiasm, and passions. Imagine you're talking to one of your close friends; trust your reader with your feelings and personality. If you approach this essay in this manner, you will be sure to have an attentive and interested audience.

Three short essays in this category are provided. Notice, first, how important these activities are to the applicants and how forcefully and interestingly that importance is conveyed. Second, notice that the uniqueness of an activity is not a prerequisite for an interesting, important, forceful response. These same characteristics are conveyed well in all three essays.

Response 1

To me, "leisure" is the time and space that is not occupied by my job. It is no less demanding or challenging than my vocation, and, indeed, it can be very integrated with my professional work. During much of my leisure time, I am actively engaged in community initiatives that address social and political issues.

My activism has traditionally followed three streams: women's issues, multiculturalism, and the arts. Sometimes, these streams merge into one, but they are always flowing in the same direction, feeding the river of social change.

I am also an avid reader of nonfiction, personal development, and spirituality books, as well as a consumer of various news resources. As a student of the art of conversation, I enjoy building relationships with others who have similar interests and diverse experiences. These relationships have broadened my perspectives and understanding of complex issues.

When time permits, I like to continue my exploration into the history of North Carolina folk arts. I am a collector and connoisseur of traditional pottery, and I am learning about the rich family heritage surrounding this art form in North Carolina.

(. . .)

Although my occupational and leisure activities occupy separate "spaces" in my life, each is informed—and transformed—by the other. My involvement with various issues and organizations has enabled me to explore diverse leadership styles, develop public communications skills, and employ critical thinking and strategic planning. I am very fortunate to have achieved a synergy between my professional and personal lives.

Response 2

For me, the one thing that brings the most enjoyment and the most fun is the pursuit of antiques. But antiques as a broad classification is not altogether accurate. I have never had the financial resources or desire to deal in rare and expensive pieces of furniture or art. The area that I find most fascinating is that which I call day-to-day trash and treasure. For as long as I can remember, the opportunity to comb through mounds of knickknacks and other old junk has been a treat. My treasures are more of what were once a part of everyday life. I usually limit my hunts to objects from the period of time between the birth of my grandparents and my own birth. This assures me a point of reference or at least someone to provide final word for those unexplainable devices. One of my favorite is a cast-iron object I found several years ago at a flea market. To me it looked more like a medieval torture device than a usable utensil. After some research at the library and discussions with older relatives, I discovered it to be a bread toaster once used on an open-hearth fireplace!

The value or the rarity of the objects that find their way into my collection has never been important to me. The real joy is in the process of discovery, both at the shop or market and of the object's original use. I think true fascination is the understanding of everyday life during the seventy-five years before my birth. They say that one man's trash is another man's treasure, and I certainly provide the treasure part of the equation and just maybe a better understanding of everyday life during the late nineteeth and early twentieth centuries.

Response 3

During the last three years, I have been involved with an activity that has changed my personality and lifestyle. Three years ago, because I was quite thin and not particularly strong, I made the decision to improve my strength and health through weight training. During the first year, I trained on my own and made minimal gains. My strength increased slightly, but I was not generating the results I wanted.

After my first year, I joined a gym and began training with a professional trainer. I began studying about all aspects of training, including diet and training techniques. My strength started to increase and an awareness arose between myself and my body. I started to understand what my body needed to grow and how to train it successfully. By the end of my second year, I had gained twelve pounds and started to become more confident in my ability. It was during my third year that I made the most significant gains. I gained twenty pounds and had developed substantial training knowledge. Proper technique is one of the most important aspects of training and I was now able to instruct others. I was aware of proper diet and had begun a diet that helped me continue to gain weight.

All aspects came together during the third year. My self-esteem increased and my academic performance increased. I had learned patience and I had learned discipline. I felt better about myself and became even more driven to succeed. My perceptions of what could be accomplished expanded. In addition, I made the decision to take weight training to the next step, sharing what I have learned with others, by committing to becoming a professionally certified trainer. Another offshoot of this interest was my being employed to design a 2,000-square-foot training facility which was completed one year ago and which has been a success.

As mentioned elsewhere in this application, I plan to enter medical school in addition to earning the MBA. What I have learned from what started out as a personal matter now has the possibility of helping me in a medical context in the long run. However, I hope that this unexpected development does not come to detract from the personal challenges, rewards, and sense of accomplishment I have enjoyed throughout my experience.

Analysis

There's no mistaking the distinctly different and uniquely interesting personalities and personal lives of the applicants. On the basis of this alone, the essays are successful. Note how each writer is unafraid to let the reader share in his or her chosen activity. Note how each writer is careful to be very detailed in describing not only the actual activity, but also his or her feelings about the activity. If you critically read each of these essays, you can detect certain highly desirable characteristics about each applicant, characteristics important to and desired in an MBA candidate. One final point to be made is that the essay on weight lifting could easily have been used for an essay on accomplishments.

Ethical Dilemmas

Before you can begin to relate an ethical dilemma you have faced, you must be clear about what is meant by *ethical* and about what the committees are seeking to measure with the answers they receive. The biggest mistake made in answering ethical dilemma questions is to confuse the terms *legal* and *ethical*. For our purposes, legal and ethical issues are not the same thing. The committee seeks to determine how far you would go in a situation in which it is unclear what is right or wrong—an area in which no official, legislated lines of conduct have been drawn. Where would you draw the line? It is your ethical judgment that the committee is seeking to measure. Insider trading, failing to comply with the terms of a contract, and embezzlement of funds are not ethical issues; they are legal issues. Nevertheless, a vast majority of applicants answer the essay by dealing with legal issues. Steer clear of situations that have clearly marked boundaries of behavior.

It is interesting to review the basis for incorporating ethical questions into the application process. These questions were added to the process because of the questionable business dealings of the 1980s and early 1990s—business dealings that were encouraged, in part, by business schools' perceived selection of greedy, uncaring individuals. Because of this perception, business schools sought to improve their image. They attempted to gauge the moral and ethical makeup of prospective MBAs by incorporating ethical inquiries into the application process. It may also be that schools began demanding more work experience of applicants because such experience helps to provide perspective on dealing with moral and ethical dilemmas. Perhaps because of the schools' responses to this situation, there has been a reduction in the number of ethical controversies reported by the media, and essay questions on this topic are now being dropped from some applications. Nevertheless, many programs still consider an applicant's ethics to be revealing of the character of that applicant, as shown in the following essay questions:

> Describe an ethical dilemma you have experienced and discuss how you handled it. (University of California at Berkeley)
>
> Describe an ethical dilemma you have experienced and how you handled the situation. (University of Florida)

These two are identical in content and focus: they require you to choose a dilemma and discuss how you reacted to it. Be advised, however, that ethical questions in the past have also asked for an explanation of how the dilemma was resolved.

In contrast, consider the following question found in the University of Indiana's application:

Assume you are a senior executive in the process of hiring a new manager. What questions would you direct to this potential employee to assess whether this person would be an ethical manager? Please justify your choice of questions.

Please notice that the question requires you to recognize an ethical dilemma, exhibit analytical skills (by knowing what questions to ask), and explain the premises upon which you selected your questions.

If the essay does not inquire about your resolution of the dilemma, you needn't worry or concern yourself with revealing your ultimate decision to the committee. In writing this type of essay, simply describe the dilemma, provide the committee with a detailed look at your thought process in evaluating the situation (citing specific alternative courses of action and why you might have considered each one), and relate anything you may have learned about yourself or business management by analyzing your ethical dilemma.

As with all essays, being honest is always the best policy; however, be sure to discuss a dilemma in which your course of action ultimately shows good instincts and judgment. Or if, in retrospect, you know that you should have handled the situation in a different, more mature fashion, then explain why your actions would now be different.

Ethical dilemma questions pose problems for most people for a variety of reasons. The biggest problem most applicants face is recognizing and addressing an ethical dilemma when one arises. If you have been fortunate enough to have avoided ethical dilemmas up to this point in your professional life, examine your personal life. You will find that you're bombarded with ethical dilemmas every day. At some point in your personal or professional life, there is sure to have been a situation in which you found yourself wondering, "What's the right thing to do?" The essential characteristic of an ethical dilemma is that it does not have an obvious solution; it consists of being caught between the proverbial "rock and a hard place." It's a safe bet that any decision that elicited a twinge of discomfort or guilt represented an ethical dilemma.

If you are absolutely at a loss for an ethical dilemma and you are totally focused on a program that has an essay on this issue, your approach may have to be somewhat creative. You might try something like, "I have been fortunate enough to have avoided ethical dilemmas; however, I can envision the potential for such a dilemma in the following situation . . . ," and go on to explain what you mean and how you would approach the situation. Try to pick a hypothetical situation that is close to your present or past experience. With a little bit of memory searching and imagination, though, you should be able to come up with at least one event or situation that presented you with an ethical problem.

Finally, you may want to consider saving this essay until last. Ethical dilemmas are touchy subjects and are certainly quite difficult to write about. Finish the more mainstream essays first, saving time to ponder your eventual approach to the ethical dilemma essays.

Other Essay Types

Painful, Difficult, Highly Challenging Experiences

A close relative of the ethical dilemma, this type of essay is a bit more lenient in that the definition of *painful* or *difficult* is entirely subjective. The admissions committees will be much more interested in what you learned from whatever experience you discuss and how it relates to and has an impact on your decision to go to business school than in the actual experience itself. This essay question is intended to provide the committee with a look at another type of experience in your background.

The advantage of this type of question is found in its ability to gain very valuable insights into the inner workings of the applicant. Consider the following essay questions:

Describe a failure and how you dealt with it. (University of Virginia)

Discuss a personal failure that had an impact on your professional practices or management style. Why do you consider the situation a failure? How did you resolve the situation? Did it change your professional outlook? If so, how? (Duke University)

Recognizing that successful leaders are able to learn from failure, describe a situation in which you failed. Why did you fail? (Harvard)

Describe an experience in which you met failure. Evaluate your performance in this circumstance. (University of Kansas)

Recognizing that effective leaders are able to learn from failure, describe a situation in which you failed. Why did you fail? What did you learn? (University of Alabama)

Discuss the most significant personal risk you've taken. What was the outcome? How did this change affect you as a person? (Duke University)

The greatest challenge I have faced . . . (Emory University)

Describe the most significant personal or professional decision-making challenge you have experienced. How did this experience affect your personal/professional development? (Pennsylvania State University)

Describe a situation from your immediate background that demonstrates how your level of motivation has allowed you to overcome an adversity. (Pennsylvania State University)

Discuss a challenge in your life, why you consider it a challenge, and what you learned. (Washington University)

Please describe a work-related conflict you faced. How did you handle the situation? (Michigan State University)

The essay for Duke University clearly presents the three-pronged approach of the ethical dilemma essay: describe the experience, discuss what you discovered about yourself and/or business management, and conclude by noting the relevance of this experience in your MBA decision.

Different versions of this approach are found in the essay questions of other schools. Harvard and University of Alabama ask you to examine why you failed. Even though Harvard does not require it, you should conclude your essay to Harvard by explaining what you learned from the experience as requested by University of Alabama. University of Kansas requests that you evaluate your performance, another way of inquiring what you learned and what you learned about yourself, a response that could also be used for University of Virginia. Penn State, in contrast to the others, focuses upon the role of your motivation in addressing and conquering adversity. The questions shown for Penn State, Michigan State, Washington University, Duke University, and Emory do not specifically mention failure.

Creative Brainbenders

Questions that fall into this category, as one would expect, span the gamut of possibilities:

"The unexamined life is not worth living"—Socrates, *The Apology*, by Plato. In light of the above quotation, please discuss a decision you have made that, in retrospect, has had a profound influence on your present circumstances. In hindsight, would you have made a different decision? Please explain. (University of California at Berkeley)

Of all the persons past and present, I would most like to meet . . . (Washington University)

Describe someone you admire and explain why you admire this person. How have you incorporated what you have learned from this individual in your life? (University of Kansas)

Suppose you had to choose three people—people alive now or people from another era—to travel with you on a cross-country automobile trip. Who would you choose and why? What would you hope to learn from them? (Indiana University)

You have the opportunity to invite three individuals who have ever lived to help solve a problem. What problem would you solve? What role would each person, including yourself, play on the team? (University of North Carolina—Chapel Hill)

These questions are designed by admissions committees in an attempt to understand your perception of the world around you, how you think, and how you see yourself fitting into that world. What you have to say is important, but more important is how you say it. The committee members want to experience your brain at work—they want to see "how your wheels turn upstairs." Thus, your strategy is to present an honest and original, well-reasoned idea and back that idea up with a sound, logical argument, using specifics as evidence. Again, clarity of expression and purpose are very important. These essays provide yet another opportunity to express your individuality, as each applicant will say something different. Attempt to provide the admissions committee with a fresh idea, and your essay will be effective.

Academics

Consider the following essay questions. Note that only Penn State's is *not* optional:

If there is any other information that is critical for us to know and is not captured elsewhere (e.g., extenuating circumstances affecting academic or work performance), please feel free to attach a separate statement of explanation. (Stanford University)

Is there anything you think the Admissions committee should know that you feel has not been covered by the rest of this application? If you believe your credentials and essays represent you fairly, do not feel obligated to answer this question. (The American Graduate School of International Management)

The Admissions Committee welcomes any additional relevant information you wish to include in support of your application. If necessary, please comment on your academic record as an indication of your potential for graduate management education and/or any unexplained gaps in your work history. If you are currently not employed full-time, please comment and provide information about your current activities. (Georgetown University)

Do you feel that your grades and/or GMAT scores adequately reflect your abilities and your readiness to commence MBA studies? If not, why not? (Pennsylvania State University)

Begin by taking into consideration the academic environment of the school posing the question. For example, it would make most sense to target a Harvard or Darden (Virginia) essay toward the case method of study because their teaching approaches are nearly entirely case method. Rather than pointing out how well you performed in college (a strategy most people employ), try instead to discuss a specific course you took in which a bit of the Socratic method of questioning (learning through example and discussion) was used, and offer your performance and enjoyment of this particular class as evidence of your ability in a case environment. Keeping in mind the essay techniques of being specific and relating all experiences to your desire to get an MBA, this approach makes sense.

Many applicants feel obligated to discuss deficient grades and/or GMAT scores in this space. Opinions vary on this subject. On the one hand, an applicant with excellent work experience, great essays, sterling recommendations, and superior GMAT scores but inferior grades may wish to explain this inconsistency, hoping to eliminate questions in the minds of the committee members. On the other hand, an applicant might not want to direct attention to a weak link, especially when grades are only one factor in the application.

If you choose to use the optional essay to discuss grades and GMAT scores, take a positive, persuasive, and proactive approach to the essay rather than make defensive excuses. In other words, provide the committee with an honest assessment of why the problem occurred, such as immaturity, having to learn to discipline yourself, or whatever and then redirect the committee's attention. Focus on evidence of your current level of maturity and commitment combined with your ability to complete the demands of the program, such as your performance during your last two years, your high GMAT score, and/or your performance in courses taken since graduation. Or, if there are particular courses in which you performed admirably, particularly those of a quantitative nature in addition to English and other communications courses, then stress these as indicators of your true ability. Be proactive rather than defensive whenever possible.

Class Diversity

This current "hot" essay topic is admittedly a difficult one on which to offer guidance because it can be multifaceted. Consider the following examples of questions:

> Identify the five (5) most significant personal and/or professional skill areas you currently possess, and explain how each will enable you to contribute to making your enrollment at TEXAS a memorable experience for both you and your fellow classmates. (To guide your response to this question, you may wish to review [our] "Competitive Application Characteristics." This list identifies many of the specific characteristics looked for by the Admission Committee during its review of your application.) (University of Texas at Austin)
>
> Define diversity in your own words. Drawing upon your definition and experience, describe the rewards and challenges of diversity. (University of Michigan)
>
> What unique international background, cross-cultural perspectives, and/or unique experiences will you bring with you to Thunderbird? (The American Graduate School of International Management)
>
> Please describe how your work experience relates to the Krannert Graduate Management program and explain the skills you bring to this program that could benefit your potential classmates. (Purdue University)
>
> My most memorable cross-cultural experience . . . (Emory University)
>
> If you are applying for admission without post-baccalaureate experience, what unique contributions can you make to the class? (Ohio State University)

One characteristic of these essay questions is that they have their own diversity. Ohio State, for example, is the first university to acknowledge that it will consider direct-entry applicants. The American Graduate School, because of its international orientation, expresses that having international experiences will be quite helpful but allows for applicants' having other unique experiences that are not international in scope. The University of Michigan takes a far different approach by asking you to describe your concept of diversity and to then place your life experiences within your own framework. Emory requires applicants to have a cross-cultural experience. Purdue assumes the position that diversity can be found in a professional environment.

Note the two distinct thrusts in these essays. The first requires you to explain how your background and experiences will add to the diversity of the class. The second asks you to speculate about how the diversity of your class will benefit you once you reenter the professional world.

On the surface, the first thrust is nothing more than the "what makes you unique" theme. Because there are many things that make you unique, which do you stress? Do you stress the particular skills—accounting, computer, psychological, or quantitative—you have developed over time? Do you stress your personal qualities such as your sense of humor, quick analytical ability, communications skills, leadership skills, and/or abilities as a facilitator or negotiator? Or do you stress the various conditions you have encountered in life that have shaped your perceptions, such as growing up in a small town or attending a very small high school where you had to learn to get along with nearly everyone; experiences in the military, a sorority, a fraternity, or other campus group; or your role in voluntary activities? Any of these characteristics are prime candidates for inclusion. Find a personal theme that will capture three or four characteristics and construct your response around that theme.

The key to the second thrust, which asks you how the diversity of your class will benefit you once you reenter the professional world, is found in the presumption that you have built a career development plan into your application. Picking three characteristics inherent in the diversity espoused for the class and showing how you will utilize them in your career development should provide the basis for your development of this type of essay.

If, for whatever reason, you are truly uncomfortable with this essay because you are unsure what it seeks to discern, then you have two choices. The first is to acknowledge in your essay that you are unclear, state the direction you are going to take and why, and proceed. The second is to read the program's literature to get a sense of what the program is stressing about the diverse nature of its class. If diversity is in fact a characteristic in which the program takes great pride, then there should be something reflecting this pride in the literature. Look for some characteristics of the diversity that is causing such pride. For guidance in this approach, refer to the suggestions found within the University of Texas essay question. If the literature doesn't provide you with any clue, then go back to what makes you unique. Pick three to four characteristics, fully develop them, and go for it.

The Optional Essay

Almost every application will give the applicant the "option" to add something further to the application. If there's one thing that the "optional" essay is not, that is optional. No single application provides you with the chance to cover every aspect of your life, but the optional essay gives you the chance to cover what you need to say but haven't yet been asked. Never omit the optional essay. Take the opportunity to reinforce and advance your persuasive argument for being admitted. You may wish to adapt an essay you wrote for another application if you feel it covers an important aspect of your background. If there's any relevant aspect of your background not covered in a particular application, use this opportunity to incorporate that aspect.

Finally, be sure to never repeat information contained in other parts of the application and always end on a positive note. Here is an optional essay that stresses the uniqueness of its author:

Response
Within this envelope is the most comprehensive package of information ever assembled about me. I have never had the opportunity or the reason to put together such a package, and in reflecting on the "experience," I come away with a certain amount of satisfaction. I have learned a great deal about myself, both by looking back at my accomplishments and academic records and by looking forward at my hopes, dreams, and aspirations.

After putting a great deal of thought into this application the one thing that has become self-evident is that no one part of this package adequately describes who I am and what I wish for the future. To look at my recommendations or work experience or academic record or extracurricular activities singularly does not describe my potential in the business world or why I should be admitted to ____. However, the thing that each of these individual pieces tells when taken together is that I have a history of success at each phase of my life. There is no doubt in my mind that this point in my life is not the end of that potential. The question for me now is "can I succeed and reach my aspirations without a graduate degree?" My answer to that thought is an emphatic "NO!" As my work experience and activities indicate, I have never wished to merely participate. With this in mind, my next step is to earn the credentials, analytical skills, broadened horizons, and general maturation that come with an MBA.

For me, that "step" is achieved at ____. After spending a few days visiting classes, talking to professors and students, and spending a great deal of time studying what other programs have to offer, I have come to realize that ____ has the most to offer me in preparing for the future. It is with these thoughts in mind that I offer to you my application for admission and an individual ready to assume the rigors and challenges of ____.

The statement ". . . I have a history of success at every phase of my life" could be interpreted either as arrogance or as an overstatement of reality. It also could squeeze the applicant into a corner: If this same application included an essay question requiring the applicant to discuss a failure, then this applicant, after making this bold statement, would have no legitimate response. There can be no doubt, however, that the essay reveals a great deal about the applicant, particularly about whether he or she will fit into the culture of the program.

What Every Essay Must Convey

Remember that admissions committee members are fond of saying, "I don't know how to describe it but I will know it when I see it." What is it that grabs the attention of committee members when they read an essay?

Of the applicants who have caught the attention of admissions committees, there have been rock and jazz musicians and orchestral performers. There have been athletes who tried to go pro but then realized that professional sports were not in their future. There have been many volunteers in all types of organizations, people giving of their time and skills after work and on weekends. There have been entrepreneurs, people who encountered rapid changes across a wide range of jobs, and employees on rapid promotion paths. What all these people have had in common is that they gave the impression of having the ability to complete and to reflect positively upon the program after completion. There is little doubt that these characteristics continue to comprise the basis for acceptance, regardless of the form in which some essay questions are posed.

The following is an excellently written essay that, with minimum modification and change in focus, could be used to respond to several different types of essay questions. This essay was written as a response to one of the self-analysis questions previously presented. Minor modifications could easily change the focus to that of a diversity essay. Some sections of it are also applicable to an Ability to Contribute in a Group essay.

Response

The person I am today is a product of twenty-three years of experiences. Throughout the course of my life, countless people and situations have contributed to my values, beliefs, and interests. My education, work, and family have provided me with a valuable opportunity to interact with people from a wide variety of backgrounds. I believe that such exposure has enabled me to be both more aware of and sensitive to the needs of others, making me a more conscientious individual.

Growing up as the daughter of a minister, I was typically at the center of a religious community largely comprised of adults. As a result, I was often required to interact on a mature level with members of the congregation, whether that meant leading part of an Advent service, visiting a nursing home, or fielding phone calls about deaths in the church. Learning to overcome the often-present age barrier was a challenge that enhanced my ability to relate to other generations.

I also owe my family gratitude for introducing me to other religions. During summer vacations, my father insisted that we attend services at churches of other sects and denominations, ranging from Greek Orthodox to Southern Baptist. Through such visits he hoped to teach us that another person's beliefs, while different from our own, can still be equally valid and meaningful. Though as a child I did not recognize the impact of such exposure, I know that those lessons carried over into my adult life, making me more open-minded and accepting. My personal scope was further expanded through my educational experiences.

The public high school I attended had a large vocational education curriculum, offering such programs as auto mechanics, cosmetology, and secretarial training. Because these classes were located in a different wing, the college preparatory students were typically only united with the vocational students in certain required courses. While these classes tended to be less challenging academically, they served as a meaningful forum for social and personal development. The friendships I formed through this interaction afforded me a respect for individuals who choose to follow paths different from my own. This has certainly served as an advantage in my work life, because I can appreciate the dedication of an administrative assistant as much as that of a top executive and the skills of a punch-press operator as much as those of a plant manager.

My local school system was also racially balanced. Thus, I encountered both the camaraderie and the tensions that can stem from a multicultural environment. Though the general student body remained relatively divided, I was active in organizations such as band and orchestra that brought people together through a common interest. This allowed us to get to know one another on a level beyond skin color and family background. At the time, I definitely did not fully realize the value of my experience. In reflection, however, I can now greatly attribute the development of my character and convictions to the diversity of my classmates. The impact of my high school experience became more evident when I enrolled at a small, private college with very few minority students or faculty members.

While at this college I found myself living and working alongside students from prestigious families, with generations of college degrees attached to their names. This was certainly a new environment for me, one that required significant adjustment. At times, I was unpleasantly reminded that my background differed from that of the typical student at this university.

Upon writing my first English paper, for example, I met with my professor. After reviewing my work, she asked where I had attended high school. Once I offered the name of my alma mater, she simply replied, "I see. We have a lot of work to do." Though I resented the implication that my prior education was any less demanding than that of my classmates, many of whom attended reputable preparatory schools, her remarks prompted me to excel in future work in order to prove my abilities.

Despite small incidents like this, the friendships I made while in college quickly convinced me that socioeconomic backgrounds need not dictate personal relationships or achievements. Instead, I found that differences between people can serve to eliminate bias and broaden perspectives, forming more well-rounded individuals.

Once I graduated, I found that my varied experiences with a multitude of people readily prepared me for life in the corporate world. This was especially apparent during my first job assignment, which required me to work on the shop floor of a manufacturing facility as a member of a consulting team. Many of the employees at the plant were significantly older than I and were not particularly receptive to the team as a whole, since many of their colleagues had recently been laid off due to downsizing efforts. I was warned that they would be even less eager to work with a young, college-educated female who had limited manufacturing experience.

At the onset of the project, I found this prediction to be quite accurate. As I introduced myself to a shipping dock employee, he flatly stated, "Why are you here? What do you know about my job?" Another proclaimed, "I don't like consultants, but I don't mind skirts." Trying to mask my discomfort and apprehension, I attempted to explain my purpose for invading their territory. I wanted them to realize that I should not be viewed as a threat, but rather as a colleague. Because much of my work depended upon the cooperation of the shop floor workers, I knew that my ability to build a productive relationship with them would significantly impact the success of the project. By relying on my past experiences and remaining sensitive to their concerns, I eventually gained the approval of the group and even forged some friendships. By the time the project came to an end, we had effectively and enjoyably worked together to complete the tasks at hand. This achievement built my confidence and allowed me to prove my worth to the engagement team.

When I moved on to my next project, I was confronted with a similar situation. Instead of building rapport with blue-collar workers, however, I was required to collaborate with international business-people. While coordinating a global manufacturing survey, I worked regularly with representatives from eleven countries, planning everything from the distribution of the survey tool to the publishing of the results. Of course, it can be difficult enough managing the opinions and expectations of eleven people, but the language barriers and cultural differences quickly compound the challenge. Issues that originally seemed insignificant often sparked great controversy between the participating countries.

During a marketing strategies conference in Paris, for instance, we attempted to settle on a graphic icon to represent the concept of quality. While the United States had planned to use a picture of calipers, the U.K. delegate requested that we use the symbol for Sterling silver. The Japanese and Italian representatives felt that neither symbol would be identifiable in their respective countries, so they offered alternate suggestions. The discussion continued for approximately two hours, until an agreement was reached. From there, the meeting remained calm, at least until we began to discuss a symbol for flexibility.

Though this was my first experience working on an international project, I believe my ability to relate to many different people was essential. The meeting confirmed that being sensitive and nonjudgmental are critical skills when working as a team, particularly when the team members are richly diverse. In addition, the project further expanded my scope and awareness of other cultures, a quality that is certain to be advantageous in future endeavors.

I expect that pursuing an MBA will allow me to expand upon my past experiences, introducing me to unique individuals and new lines of thought. I believe that ___ can provide the means through which I may continue to broaden my knowledge and perspectives. I also feel that my background, values, and outlook can contribute to the wealth of diversity found in the business school community.

I recognize that my personal development is far from complete. As I tackle new challenges, meet new people, and confront extraordinary situations, my character will continually be shaped. I welcome the growth that will undoubtedly occur.

Analysis

You will not have had the same experiences found in this essay; you will, however, have had a wealth of your own. Accordingly, do not be intimidated by this essay but instead enjoy it and learn from it. This essay conveys some rather commonplace situations in an impressive fashion. For example, the experiences relating to both the high school and the small college are rather typical but, as told, it effectively communicates a very positive image of the author's uniqueness. Conveying some of the values instilled through parental relationships also says a great deal about the author. Reconciling differences of opinion or overcoming hostilities is nothing new; doing so in a foreign country or in a consulting capacity is more unusual. What is most interesting, however, is the author's openness about her experiences. You might want to reread this essay paragraph by paragraph and component by component for the purpose of triggering images and ideas that you can then turn into an equally forceful essay for yourself.

A Final Thought

Writing essays for business school applications is an intensely intro-spective and exhausting experience. One realistically possible conse-quence of that experience is the gaining of new perspectives along the way. If you keep this thought in mind when answering the many essay questions that you will face, you will have the proper frame of mind for writing the essays. Should those perspectives arise, you will find the reward to be most fulfilling.

9

The Structure, Scoring, and Grading of the GMAT

You may be tempted to skip this section since your objective is to maximize your score on the GMAT regardless of how it is administered, structured, or graded. While this temptation may be understandable, it is shortsighted. You should be as familiar with the GMAT process as with the application process. Understanding the respective characteristics of the exam will enable you to appreciate the strategies for improving your score recommended in the next chapter.

This section has been kept brief intentionally and you are encouraged to invest the few minutes required to learn about test scheduling (and taking advantage of that scheduling), exam structure, question format and content, and the grading of the exam. Once you have completed these few pages, you will be better prepared for the material that follows.

Getting Started

The GMAT is one of several standardized entrance examinations written and published by Educational Testing Service (ETS). The test is administered by the Graduate Management Admissions Council (GMAC). To begin the testing process, you need to obtain copies of the *GMAT Information Bulletin* and *The Official Guide for GMAT Review*, and log onto the GMAT Web site at http//www.gmat.org. Available at this site are listings of testing sites and phone numbers, sample test questions, representative essay topics, and other information about the GMAT itself. This site also contains an order form for test preparation and software material, financial aid information, schedules for forums, information on MBA programs and careers, and other MBA publications. Finally, information on approximately 500 business schools and Internet links to over 350 schools is provided.

One of the quickest ways to get the GMAT bulletin is to go to the MBA office or perhaps the career planning and placement office on the nearest college campus. Or you can call ETS at 609-771-7330.

The GMAT Is in the Computer Age

Computers and the GMAT are now inseparable. The exam's two multiple-choice and two essay sections are now administered using computers at designated sites. Upon completion of the computerized exam, you instantaneously receive your multiple-choice scores. Your scores on the two essay sections are reported one to two weeks later. You leave knowing how you performed in the quantitative and verbal sections and presumably leave feeling good about your score because you prepared for the exam by using the guidance and directions found in the next chapter.

On-Site Conditions and Preparation

The environment and conditions are advertised as being controlled, businesslike, and conducive to taking the exam. Some test takers have commented, however, that the sheer level of activity can be disturbing. You are allowed to use only the material and equipment made available to you at the testing center—an arrangement of work stations with the computer system and pencils and paper for making notations. Other material, referred to as *test aids, including a calculator*, is prohibited.

Tutorials are provided to familiarize you with the mouse-based computer system's characteristics. You have time to practice using the system prior to beginning the exam. It is strongly suggested that at home before the exam you thoroughly familiarize yourself with the suggested reference materials and that you arrive at the testing center at least half an hour before your scheduled exam so that you have time to get to know the system.

You select multiple-choice answers with a click of a mouse. You must confirm your answer before you are able to move on to the next question. The essay sections require knowledge of basic word processing features: cut, paste, undo, backspace, and delete, as well as cursor movement. A spell-check feature is not available. Highlights of the computer screens and operating system are found in the *GMAT Information Bulletin, The Official Guide for GMAT Review*, and other GMAT references.

When to Take the GMAT

Conventional wisdom suggests that the earlier you take the exam the better. First and foremost, this enables you to complete the application process and to get your file into the hands of the committee earlier, a good strategy for those programs with large applicant pools. Additionally, it may give the committee the impression that you have planned ahead and have taken an organized approach to the application process.

If you want to wait until the very last minute, a window of time from September through December is open. Many business schools make their initial admissions decisions in January. Most application deadlines occur in March or April, which means that a March test date allows no room for error and may not reach the admissions committee in time. This late in the cycle, nearly all of the seats available, scholarship support, and assistantships will have been assigned, drastically reducing the probability of your being accepted.

Another limitation that must be acknowledged is that the later you take the exam, the less time you will have to recover should you need to retake the GMAT. For example, if you take the exam in October, you have no more than two months to retake the exam. During this time you must discern what caused your less-than-desired GMAT performance and take corrective action. Be advised that you can take the GMAT only once in any given month.

If you are really thinking ahead you should consider taking the exam some six to twelve months before you begin the application process (twelve to eighteen months before you intend to enroll). If your scores are on target, then you can put the exam behind you and focus on school selection and application strategy.

Structure and Format

There are four separate sections of the exam: Analysis of an Issue, Analysis of an Argument, Quantitative Reasoning, and Verbal Section. These are to be completed within a period of approximately four and one-half hours.

The first section, Analysis of an Issue, and the second section, Analysis of an Argument, are part of the Analytical Writing Assessment. This is devoted to assessing your analytical writing skills and consists of two thirty-minute essay sections. Your objective is to critique the strength of the arguments made in each section.

The remaining two sections are multiple-choice questions driven by Computer Adaptive Testing (CAT). This approach determines your score by finding the highest-level question that you can answer correctly. As long as you answer correctly, CAT continues to ask you more and more difficult questions. When you select an incorrect answer, CAT adjusts to a lower level and begins to ask you questions that are easier but become more challenging as you progress. Whenever you make a mistake, CAT automatically readjusts to a lower level. From this process comes one of your first exam strategies: it is important for you to take slightly more time answering the first eight to ten questions in order to increase the likelihood of your answering correctly. Doing so locks you into a higher test score. Another feature of CAT is that once you leave a question, you cannot return to it for any reason. Therefore, it is of even greater importance to focus more on the earlier questions in order to establish your exam score positioning.

The first CAT section of the test is Quantitative Reasoning, which contains two types of questions. Problem Solving questions ask you to apply mathematical formulas and concepts to determine singular, numerical answers. Data Sufficiency gives you two informational statements and asks you to determine whether a certain conclusion can be reached using only one of the statements, either of the statements, only the two statements combined, or whether a conclusion cannot be reached from the data provided. There are thirty-seven questions and seventy-five minutes (about two minutes each) allotted to this section.

The last section, the Verbal Section, consists of Reading Comprehension, Critical Reasoning, and Sentence Correction. The structure and content of these questions should be familiar to you as they reflect the many achievement tests you have taken. Forty-one questions allotted about one and one-half minutes each (a total of seventy-five minutes) comprise this section. Answer strategies for this section are explored and explained in the next chapter.

Other Considerations

No prior knowledge of business or other specific areas is presumed. Also, within each of the multiple-choice sections are experimental questions that will be included and scored in some future exam but that will not count in your score. Because they cannot be identified, you have to complete all questions as though they are being scored.

The Analytical Writing
Assessment Sections

These two sections are the first ones you will be faced with when you start to take the GMAT. The first is Analysis of an Issue in which you are presented with an issue open to debate. You are to then adopt and support a position relative to the issue. In the second section, Analysis of an Argument, you are presented with an argument made by someone else and expected to evaluate that argument. In your response you should evaluate such characteristics as the logic of the argument, the development of the argument in terms of its reasoning, the strength of the evidence used, and the ways in which the argument could be improved.

How the Analytical Writing Assessment Section Is Scored

Only one composite (average) score is reported for the two sections even though each section is graded on a 0 through 6 scale and each is based on the assessment of at least two evaluators per section. A score of 6 is excellent, while a score of zero is assigned to those written responses that are deemed by the evaluators (ETS uses the term *reader*) as either incapable of being evaluated or as not having addressed the assigned topic. Scores are reported in half-point increments between these two extremes.

The single score reported is an average of the scores assigned to the two respective sections. These two section scores are the averages of two evaluative scores given for each section. For example, if you averaged 4.5 on one section and 5.5 on the second, then your single or composite reported score would be 5.0. Stated another way, the single score reported is essentially the average of the scores assigned by the four evaluators.

ETS maintains that procedures are in place in the grading process to ensure evaluations (scores) are fair and consistent. It claims to take steps to ensure that the overall quality represented by a score is consistent even though styles of writing, thinking, and organization differ. In other words, responses receiving the same score should demonstrate the same level of writing competency.

The Multiple-Choice Sections

Each multiple-choice question contains five choices from which you are to select the best answer. In reality, your objective is to select that answer that represents the preferred response as designated by ETS and the GMAC. The multiple-choice sections contain a total of seventy-eight questions attempting to measure your quantitative and verbal skills. You will be asked five different types of questions, two of which relate to your quantitative aptitude and three of which investigate your verbal skills.

Math Skills

Problem Solving and Data Sufficiency comprise the thirty-seven multiple-choice questions in this section. The intent of these questions is to test your ability to reason and to solve quantitative problems.

Problem Solving

The Problem Solving questions are perhaps the most straightforward ones in the GMAT: You're given a math problem and asked to solve it. About half of the questions are straight computational questions, and the rest are verbal, "real world" word problems. GMAT math covers arithmetic, elementary algebra, and geometry—nothing beyond ninth-grade math. This is good news and bad news for most people. On the one hand, it is comforting to know that the concepts tested are very basic; on the other hand, trying to recall one's junior high school math can be a battle.

Data Sufficiency

The name *Data Sufficiency* says it all. The questions in this section test your ability to analyze a quantitative problem and determine when enough information exists to solve it. It's logic and math at the same time: Math is the concept, logic is the format.

This section is very different from all other sections in design because the format for each and every question is exactly the same. Your task is not to answer the actual question asked; it is to classify the questions according to predefined classification categories. In this section, each question presents two statements. You must choose your response from the same five options every time.

Verbal Skills

The three sections testing verbal skills are Reading Comprehension, Critical Reasoning, and Sentence Correction. The objective of the forty-one questions in these sections is to test your ability to understand and evaluate reading material and to recognize basic elements of English.

Reading Comprehension

If you've ever taken a standardized entrance exam before (such as the SAT), you'll recognize the GMAT Reading Comprehension section, which is equivalent to reading comprehension on any other standardized test you have taken. Questions in this section are distributed among three different topics in reading passages approximately 300 to 350 words in length. One passage is from the natural sciences, one from the social sciences, and one from business-related fields such as economics, marketing, or the management of human resources. The only element they have in common is that they are all dry, dense, boring, and not the kind of thing you are likely to read for fun. The questions measure your ability to understand, analyze, and apply the information and concepts contained in the passages. All of the questions are to be answered on the basis of the passage, so there is no need for you to have either prior or specific knowledge of the material.

Critical Reasoning

The Critical Reasoning section is quite similar to the Reading Comprehension section. It requires many of the same skills but concentrates more on reasoning skills and the logical structure of a short argument. (In Reading Comprehension, you are given much longer "arguments" and asked a wider variety of questions.) The questions in this section test your ability to read critically, and make and evaluate arguments. Most of the questions are based on an argument, debate, short reading passage, or set of logical statements. Most of the material is drawn from the realm of business in an attempt to gauge your facility with the material you will be faced with in business school. From this standpoint alone, most test takers find this section easier to handle and somewhat more enjoyable than Reading Comprehension.

Sentence Correction

Sentence Correction may be viewed simply as a quiz on standard written English and is basically an editing exercise. The questions require you to be familiar with stylistic conventions and grammatical rules and to demonstrate your ability to improve written expressions that are either ineffective or incorrect. The goal here is to gauge your writing ability.

In each question, you are given a sentence, part or all of which is underlined. If an error in grammar or style exists, it exists only in the portion of the sentence which is underlined. Five different versions of the underlined portion of the sentence are offered as answer choices, and your task is to pick the choice that does the very best job of expressing the intended meaning of the original sentence.

How the Multiple-Choice Sections Are Scored

The overall GMAT score is on a scale of 200 to 800, with 800 being the highest. Few people score over 700 or below 350. In addition to the overall scaled score, you will receive two numerically scaled scores for the math and the verbal sections. Everyone's attention, however, is directed to the percentage score for each section because it is quickly and easily understood, reporting the percentage of the test-taking population that scored below you.

GMAT Computer Adaptive Testing (GMAT CAT)

Computer Adaptive Testing differs from traditional multiple-choice tests of aptitude and ability. The traditional approach is to ask the test taker a number of questions with varying degrees of difficulty. One point is assigned for each correct answer, a penalty is possibly assessed for each incorrect answer, and no change in score is made for an unanswered question. The test taker's final score is based on the number of correct responses. No allowance is made for differences in the degree of difficulty of the correctly answered questions. That is, a point is added to the test taker's score regardless of whether the question answered was easy, very difficult, or somewhere in between.

Correction of this perceived weakness in the traditional multiple-choice test has been addressed by ETS and GMAC and has resulted in the concept now called Computer Adaptive Testing (CAT). The process begins with a database in which multiple-choice questions have been classified by content and by degree of difficulty. The process ends with a score that takes into consideration the degree of difficulty of the questions answered correctly and the number of questions answered correctly and incorrectly. A complex formula is then applied to produce a score that is purported to reflect the level of your ability in verbal and quantitative concepts when compared with the ability of others who have taken the GMAT. One consequence of this approach is that increasingly higher scores are earned by consistently answering questions of increasing difficulty. Stated another way, more points are earned by correctly answering questions of greater difficulty.

The term *adaptive* in the name refers to the process the computer uses to select the next question, a process that considers the correctness of the question just answered, the degree of difficulty of that question, and the degree of difficulty and the number of correctly and incorrectly answered questions to that point. If your response is correct, then the next question selected will be of a higher degree of difficulty. An incorrect response results in your next question being of a lower degree of difficulty. The first question presented to you is one that has been classified as being of medium difficulty. As you continue to answer questions, the computer will select questions which represent the level of difficulty that characterizes your demonstrated ability. By the end of the examination, the computer will have established a "difficulty" profile for you to which a score is assigned.

Parting Comments

The format and structure of the respective sections are constant. Each section has a set of instructions that do not change from one exam to the next. Your objective is to familiarize yourself with the instructions and the format for each section in advance so that during the exam you can use all your time for answering questions. Your objective is to maximize your exam performance; making the effort to familiarize yourself with the content and instructions is a very small price to pay to achieve that objective!

10

Maximizing Your GMAT Performance

The GMAT is an important challenge. In this chapter, we will consider how to best prepare for this challenge. This chapter covers test preparation alternatives, test-taking strategies, and ways to maximize your GMAT scores. This discussion by no means is meant to compete with or replace any preparatory method or material, nor is it meant to be a comprehensive and definitive treatise on taking the exam. To the contrary, you are strongly encouraged—in fact, implored—to utilize resources specifically developed to improve your performance, incorporating the suggestions offered here.

Even if you are extremely good at taking standardized tests, you must take the time to familiarize yourself with the idiosyncrasies of the GMAT. For most people, a preparation period of six to eight weeks is optimal, assuming that you spend at least two hours each day preparing for the exam. One thing is certain: You will perform much better on the GMAT if you are at ease with the structure and nature of the test than you will if you take it without preparation.

Regardless of your preparation plan, your first step is to buy *The Official Guide for GMAT Review*. It is published each year by ETS— the people who write the GMAT—and is the only source of actual GMAT material. If you can, secure older editions as well so that you can practice on additional sets of multiple-choice questions.

Words of Wisdom Before You Begin

Before you get started, you must understand a few things about standardized test taking and preparation. Further, you must set specific goals based on these principles.

The first and most important principle to remember when studying to take a standardized test is that "The test maker is always right!" The sooner you realize this, the sooner you will be on your way to becoming an improved test taker. Remember, your sole goal on the exam is to get a point out of each question. Realizing that the test maker is always right will enable you to adopt the proper frame of mind. Your goal is not to point out why you think your answer is better than the credited one. Your goal is to figure out which answer the test maker prefers so you can get a point for it. The test maker has given you the credited answer—all you have to do is find it among the four decoys. This attitude requires a bit of intellectual humility and ego sublimation on your part, but it allows you to perform well on the GMAT.

The second principle you must be aware of is that, although each question is worth the same amount (one point), all questions are not of equal difficulty. The discussion in the prior chapter on Computer Adaptive Testing (CAT) forcefully emphasizes this principle. Those who quickly realize this and capitalize on it will score the highest on the GMAT. You must be able to work through a given section of the test in a way that enables you to achieve the maximum score. In the multiple-choice section of the CAT, getting as many of the first eight to ten questions right that you can will positively influence your score. No business school in the world will ask you how you did in your GMAT preparation. The only score that counts is the one you get back from ETS, so steer clear of simply gauging your performance by your practice scores.

Closely related to this second principle is the third: The GMAT rewards the mover, not the plodder. Timing is important. You must make the effort in your study to move through the questions as quickly and as efficiently as you can. Make sure you divide your time wisely on a section and stick to a schedule. Far too many test takers ignore timing. You must realize that anyone can do well on the test, given enough time. Knowing your strengths and weaknesses will help you shave off precious seconds of time as you prepare. By test day you should be able to glance at a question and know instantly whether or not to attempt it. You never want to find yourself ninety seconds into a math question (all that's allotted) and discover that you can't do the problem. Once again, focus on improving your timing.

The fourth GMAT principle to think about as you begin your study concerns guessing. A random-guessing penalty exists, so never guess randomly. However, if you can eliminate some of the wrong answer choices, or even only one, the odds of selecting the preferred answer increases. As you go through your practice, try to determine how good you are at making educated guesses and try to discern ways to improve your guessing ability. Try to focus on subtle distinctions that cause the test maker to prefer one response to another. Try to track your success and failure rate by the number of possible answer choices remaining. In other words, track the percentage of the questions you get right on the practice exams when you guess at one of two remaining possible answer choices.

If you keep these principles in mind, your assault on the GMAT should be very effective. Consider practicing on one section at a time, spending more time on those sections that give you the most trouble. In other words, don't practice taking full-length GMAT exams at first. Work on Reading Comprehension one day, Problem Solving the next, and so on. As you begin to understand where your inherent abilities lie, you can restructure your preparation so that you place more emphasis on the weaker areas.

Here again are the two steps to take as you begin to prepare for the GMAT:

1. Prepare. Plan on averaging at least two hours a day for a period of at least six to eight weeks.

2. At the very minimum, procure a copy of *The Official Guide for GMAT Review*.

Now here are the four principles underlying a successful strategy for taking the GMAT:

1. The test maker is always right.

2. All questions are worth the same amount of points but not all are of equal difficulty. Concentrate on getting the first eight to ten questions correct.

3. Move quickly in each section because speed is rewarded.

4. Never guess randomly. The greater the number of responses that can be eliminated, the greater the likelihood of your selecting the preferred answer.

Preparation Course or Self-Study?

Knowing that you should prepare is one thing; developing a strategy for preparing is another. Regardless of the preparation strategy you adopt, you are encouraged to use the hints and suggestions provided in the remainder of this chapter as your preparation proceeds. They have been provided to help you to maximize your GMAT performance.

Recall that you should plan to spend an average of two hours per day over a six- to eight-week period preparing for taking the GMAT. How committed to the concept of preparation and how disciplined are you? If you are highly committed and if you are highly disciplined, then the "strategy scales" are tipped in favor of self-preparation. If you are not, then you should consider a formal preparation course. Such courses provide structure, both in the established meeting times and in approaches to taking the test. The price you have to pay to enroll is a built-in incentive for you to take full advantage of all the features the course has to offer.

How Much Money Are You Willing to Invest in the Review Process?

For self-study, you will need to invest in, in addition to this book and the *GMAT Review*, at least one or two other GMAT preparation guides, which can then be supplemented with commercial math and grammar reviews. Your total investment should be no more than one hundred dollars. The cost for a commercial course is much higher. (Check with the respective firms regarding their "scholarship" opportunities and apply for all of them, regardless of your financial situation. Your chance of receiving some reduction in cost is greater than you think.) Local state universities and community colleges, which may offer preparation courses in an intermediate cost range, should also be investigated.

What Is Your Performance Target for the Exam?

How well do you normally do on standardized exams? How competitive are the programs to which you are seeking admission? If you have
a high performance target, are planning to apply to the very competitive programs, and tend to have problems with standardized exams,
then the probability scales may be slightly tipped in favor of the prep
courses. Then again, the prep courses cannot do anything for you that
you cannot do for yourself. However, if you need external motivation,
there is some evidence that the prep courses can help increase your
score. Some, for example, will publicize that, on average, they will
increase scores by a certain number of points. What you need to
know is that such numbers are generally based on the difference
between the scores earned by enrollees taking a simulated exam at
the very beginning of the course and their scores on a simulated exam
at the end of the course.

Note the term *simulated*. Prep centers do not use actual GMAT
material. They can't. GMAT tests are not disclosed, and they are copy-
righted to prevent anyone from using them for profit purposes.
Instead, the material used by prep courses is written by college math
and English majors, which means that the material only approximates
the questions on the GMAT. The bottom line is that the reported point
increases are proxies for exam performance improvement, not true
reflections of GMAT results. The admissions committees of some
MBA programs presume that if your score improves significantly
when you retake the exam, the first forty or fifty points of that
improvement are the result of either your taking a prep course or of
your taking the exam already. These same programs do not ask you
whether you took a prep course if you did extremely well the first time
you took the GMAT. Several prep courses have been in existence for
years; one might expect that they have developed at least some strategies that would help you to improve your GMAT performance. No one
knows the degree of that improvement, however.

If the commercial courses have the potential to improve your score,
then this same potential must exist for the courses offered by state
universities and community colleges. Investigate the consistency of a
ɔurse before you enroll. What review material are they using; how
   s it developed? How familiar with and how experienced in pre-
    ʻing the material are the presenters? How long has the course been
     ʻd, and what has been the historical evaluation of the course?

Obtaining the names and opinions of individuals who have recently completed the course is strongly recommended.

Do You Need Direct Personal Help to Review Quantitative and Verbal Material?

If you need personal help, someone to guide you and to work directly with you, then you might want to consider enrolling in a relevant math or basic English course at your local university. Combine dedicated self-study with this focused study and you have the potential to derive the same benefits as you would from a commercial prep course at a lower cost.

Regardless of the approach you take, you should be prepared to work hard in order to score well on the GMAT. Even if you do enroll in a preparation course, you should be prepared to do extra work outside the classroom. At a minimum, you will still need to purchase a copy of *The Official Guide for GMAT Review* because it is the only source of actual GMAT exams, exams that you can take during the last week of preparation for the "real one."

How to Use the Remainder of This Chapter

There are three major sections remaining in this chapter. The first two present specific tips and strategies for addressing each of the sections of the GMAT. The third presents a schedule and strategy for the two weeks leading up to the day of the exam.

Acquaint yourself with the next two sections by skimming the material and noting the respective topics. Then, when you gather your material and decide which test section to focus on first, return to the appropriate section. For example, if you are beginning to prepare for Sentence Correction, study the hints and strategies provided for that topic. Then work on the sentence correction material in your supplemental references. After becoming familiar with the content and structure of each test section, return to the strategy sections. At that point, those suggestions will become even more meaningful. Your reference material will also likely have its own set of suggestions. Use both sets. Think about what is being recommended. Integrate the recommendations and things should begin to click.

Read the last section of this chapter now so that you can anticipate what you will need to accomplish during the last two weeks of your preparation. Then, when the beginning of that period arrives, return, review, and implement the strategies suggested for a rewarding GMAT experience.

The Verbal Skills Section

Reading Comprehension

The questions in this section are distributed among three reading passages approximating 300 to 350 words in length. You'll see one passage from the natural sciences, one from the social sciences, and one from a business-related field such as economics, marketing, or the management of human resources. You must work quickly and accurately to score well on this section. The questions basically measure your ability to understand, analyze, and apply information and concepts contained in the passages. All of the questions are to be answered on the basis of the passage, so you need no previous or specific knowledge of the material.

There are six basic question types in Reading Comprehension. The first and perhaps easiest type of question tests your ability to grasp the "big picture," or main thesis, of the passage. A second question type asks you to draw an inference from facts and implications made in the passage—to read between the lines, if you will. Yet a third type of question tests your ability to understand the logical relationships between the important points and ideas in the reading passage; for example, you'll be asked to determine the strong and/or weak points of the author's presentation. A fourth type of question requires you to locate and interpret details, facts, and statements made in the passage. A fifth type of question tests your ability to apply the main idea of the passage to another situation—to extrapolate. A sixth type of question asks you to characterize the author's writing style and tone.

Strategy

The key strategy in Reading Comprehension is to recognize and extract important and necessary information in an efficient and effective manner. Consider why you normally read. Usually, it's either to learn something or for pleasure. Neither of these reasons applies to GMAT Reading Comprehension. The very worst thing you can do is simply read a passage in normal, everyday fashion and then attempt to answer the questions. You have only one purpose to consider in this type of reading: to get a point for each question. Therefore, you must read in a different way than you normally do. Here are some Reading Comprehension tips:

1. You will perform much better on passages with which you have some association. For example, if you were a science major in college, you will have a greater facility with the science passage. The material will be more familiar to you and your comprehension greater. Therefore, take a few seconds to glance at each passage before you actually begin your work and plan an order of attack based on your own background.

2. Look at the questions accompanying the passage first. Remember, your goal is to extract information that the test maker thinks is important. Only the information required by the questions is of concern to you. What better way to structure your reading strategy than to have some idea of what you will be asked? Spend about fifteen to thirty seconds skimming the questions before actually starting to read the passage.

3. Read carefully until you locate the author's main point. It almost always occurs in the first quarter of the passage. The main idea is the key that unlocks the passage. If you can't find it, you can't complete Reading Comprehension. A large percentage of the questions directly and indirectly deal with the main idea. The main idea is the big picture, so to speak—the point of which the person writing the passage wants to convince you. It sums up the evidence and facts presented. Each passage has a main idea, either explicitly stated or implied. Whichever the case may be, find that idea or thesis as quickly as possible.

4. Don't read every word. Once you find the main idea, the remainder of your reading should be a cursory mapping out of the structure of the passage. Try simply to get a general "feel" for the layout and development of the passage on a paragraph-by-paragraph basis. That way you can refer back to the necessary paragraph and examine it in detail when working on a

particular question. Far too many people waste time reading the passage carefully the first time through, taking notes as they do. Remember, you're not trying to learn anything! Simply noting the topic of each paragraph and assigning it a sequential paragraph number on the note paper provided is far more beneficial. It allows you to locate reading material quickly when and if you are required to do so by one of the questions. Do not memorize details—note their location and move on.

5. Don't waste time. Note taking wastes time. It gives you the illusion of getting something done. Mental paraphrasing and strategic word notation for reference purposes are much more effective strategies.

6. Don't spend more than eight minutes on any passage. Each passage has some easy questions attached to it, and you'll miss out on these easy points if you stubbornly waste time trying to answer more difficult questions in another section. Your objective is to score the maximum number of points.

Critical Reasoning

Critical Reasoning entails many of the same skills used in Reading Comprehension but concentrates more on reasoning skills and the logical structure of a short argument (in Reading Comprehension, you are given much longer "arguments" and asked a wider variety of questions). These questions test your ability to read critically, evaluate arguments, and reach conclusions. Most of the questions are based on a separate argument, debate, short reading passage, or set of logical statements. Most of the material is drawn from the realm of business in an attempt to gauge your facility with material similar in nature to what you will face in business school.

Three basic types of questions exist in the Critical Reasoning section. The first type of question refers to logical argument construction. You will be asked to recognize and identify the basic structure of an argument, properly drawn conclusions, underlying assumptions, and parallels in reasoning. The second type of question tests your ability to evaluate the logic of a particular argument or piece of reasoning. It will also test your ability to recognize factors that would strengthen or weaken the argument, reasoning errors made in constructing an argument, and aspects of the argumentative methodology. The third type of question requires you to construct and evaluate plans of action. Issues addressed here include the efficacy of a proposed plan, ways in which the plan could be strengthened, and the role of assumptions inherent in the plan.

Strategy

The strategies involved in answering this type of question are similar to those associated with Reading Comprehension. The major distinction is that the emphasis is on logical argumentation. Therefore, your strategy must be to identify the logical structure underlying each argument. There are three components to a Critical Reasoning argument: evidence or supporting facts, a conclusion or main idea, and an underlying assumption that ties the supporting facts to the conclusion. This structure is no different from the structure of Reading Comprehension passages; it's simply easier to analyze in a shorter argument. Each question will address one of these components, and with not much practice you'll become quite adept at identifying those components. As suggested for Reading Comprehension, quickly review the questions first.

Sentence Correction

Sentence Correction may be viewed simply as a quiz on standard written English. It basically is an editing exercise. The questions require you to be familiar with stylistic conventions and grammatical rules and to demonstrate your ability to improve ineffective or incorrectly written expressions. The goal here is to gauge your writing ability.

Each question consists of a sentence, part or all of which is underlined. If an error in grammar or style exists, it exists only in the underlined portion of the sentence. Five different versions of the underlined portion of the sentence are then offered as answer choices, and your task is to pick the choice that does the very best job of expressing the intended meaning of the original sentence.

If you learn what ETS considers a good sentence, you will have gone a long way to conquering this section. A good sentence, in the eyes of ETS, has two broad characteristics: correct expression and effective expression. A correct expression is grammatically and structurally sound. It conforms to all the rules of standard written English, such as subject-verb agreement, noun-pronoun agreement, and verb tense and pronoun consistency. An effective expression conveys an idea or relationship clearly and concisely as well as grammatically. This means that there are no superfluous words or needlessly complicated constructions in the best choice. (This does not mean, however, that the choice with the fewest or simplest words is necessarily the best choice.) Also, effective expressions use proper diction—you must be able to recognize whether the words are well chosen, accurate, and suitable for the context of the sentence.

Strategy

This section is very straightforward and also lends itself to a process-of-elimination strategy. Use this straightforward, seven-step strategy based on the design of the section:

1. Read the original sentence, identifying any flaws in grammar or style in the underlined portion. (Do not assume there is an error; about 20 percent of the questions have no errors.)

2. Before looking at the answer choices, mentally correct the errors in the underlined portion or make short notations on scratch paper. Try, however, to minimize the use of this latter strategy because of its rapid consumption of time.

3. Look at all the choices except (A)—it is a repeat of the original underlined portion. To read it would be a waste of precious time.

4. Look for errors within the four remaining choices. Eliminate those that have identifiable errors.

5. From the remaining responses pick the answer choice that represents the clearest, most concise, and most grammatically and stylistically correct expression of the original idea.

6. Read the potential answer with the original sentence. Do not neglect this step. Many times an answer choice may sound correct on its own but when combined with the rest of the sentence it becomes incorrect.

7. If the situation in step 6 arises, carefully reconsider the original structure as the preferred choice. About one in five (20

percent) of the original sentences is the preferred choice in the eyes of ETS.

The Math Skills Section

Problem Solving

In the questions designated for Problem Solving, you are given math problems and asked to solve them. About half of the questions are straight mathematical problems, and the rest are verbal, real world word problems. GMAT math covers arithmetic, elementary algebra, and geometry—nothing beyond ninth-grade math.

This is good news and bad news for most people. On the one hand, it is comforting to know that the concepts tested are very basic. On the other, trying to recall junior high school math can be a battle. This is why preparation is so important for this section.

For example, engineers, as a group, have some of the strongest mathematical skills in the nation. Given their ability relative to the rest of the population, one would presume that individuals with strong engineering backgrounds would have the top scores in the math skills area. Not so. Scores in the eightieth percentile (and even lower) are much more common than one would expect. This is because so much time has passed since the test takers first learned the concepts covered in the quantitative sections. One test taker, an engineer, was overheard telling another after the exam that he hadn't been able to remember a formula so he took the time to derive it. Impressive, but a sheer waste of time! This ability does not show up in the final scores.

Strategy

GMAT math is much different than high school math. The GMAT math questions do not test knowledge of concepts as much as they test one's cleverness with a few basic concepts. The intuitive test taker will likely do much better than the number cruncher. Often, a quick glance at the answer choices before you begin blindly writing and solving equations will provide you with all the insight you need. Make every effort to take no more than one and one-half minutes for each question.

Data Sufficiency

The second type of question in the math section is called Data Sufficiency, and the name says it all. The questions in this section test your ability to analyze a quantitative problem and to determine when enough relevant information exists to solve it. Math is the concept, logic is the format.

The Data Sufficiency question has a design that is very different from all other questions. Your task is not to answer each question asked, but to classify each question according to the same five categories.

Strategy

Instead of answering the actual question posed, as in all other GMAT test questions, you must classify the additional, supporting information given according to the predefined classifications. The following straightforward method is quite effective:

1. Determine what is being asked. Two types of questions exist in this section: "yes or no" questions and "calculation" questions (for example, "Is Mitchell taller than Tara?" and "How tall is Mitchell?"). An actual answer to the "yes or no" question will be *yes* or *no*. Calculation questions will have a number for an actual answer. (Keep in mind that you are not really concerned with actual answers—this step simply provides a good starting point.)

2. Spend a few seconds thinking about the kind of information you need to answer the question. This will help you when you actually begin analyzing the supplied information.

3. Analyze the two separate data statements to decide whether they are sufficient to yield one and only one answer to the question. (This is the definition of *sufficient*. Information is insufficient if more than one answer to the question is possible.) A key strategy, one ignored by most GMAT test takers, is to examine the two data statements separately. First, if you want, write 1 and 2 on the notepaper provided for you. Then completely

ignore data statement 2 and analyze data statement 1. Place a small *i* (for insufficient) or *s* (for sufficient) next to the number 1 on your paper. Then do the same with data statement 2 while blocking statement 1 from your mind. To repeat, you must completely erase data statement 1 from your mind when working with 2. In most cases, you will have automatically rendered the correct answer by this point.

4. If you discover that you have two insufficient pieces of data, you must now combine them to see if together they provide an answer to the question.

Three major errors are made by test takers in this section:

1. Being predisposed to finding an answer of "yes" to a "yes or no" question. Many people confuse *sufficiency* with a "yes" answer. The two are not synonymous. Similarly, a "no" answer does not mean *insufficient*. "No" is a perfectly acceptable and sufficient answer to a "yes or no" question.

2. Doing too much work. Do only as much calculation and analysis as needed to determine whether a single answer can or cannot be obtained. Remember, you are simply trying to classify the sufficiency of the supplied data statements; you are not trying to answer the question posed.

3. Not following this commonsense method. For example, many test takers will mistakenly keep data statement 1 in mind when analyzing data statement 2. This directly opposes the prescribed method and will most certainly lead to error.

Summary

Throughout the course of your preparation, constantly keep track of your individual strengths and weaknesses. It is only by taking this qualitative approach that you will truly become a wise test taker. Keep noting the kinds of things you consistently get correct, the kinds of questions you struggle with, and the kinds of questions you find nearly impossible to answer. In this way, when it comes time to take the test you can work through a section, answering questions that match your strengths, thereby ensuring you a top score. Do not spend too much time on any one question, especially after the first ten. By that point the computerized adaptive process will have started to "firmly classify" you at a particular level of ability. Your objective is to get as many questions answered "correctly" as you can in the remaining time. Learning your strengths and weaknesses enables you to avoid wasting time while working toward that maximum score that reflects your capabilities.

The Analytical Writing Assessment Section

Analytical Writing Assessment has two sections: Analysis of an Issue and Analysis of an Argument. The general format and content of the two sections are quite similar and the manner in which your performance will be evaluated will reflect that similarity. Both have as their overall objective the assessment of your ability to critically analyze and then effectively express your thoughts in writing on debatable issues. In the first section, you are asked to present your position on an issue; in the second, you are presented with a position being espoused by another person and asked to critically analyze and evaluate that position. Your abilities to think critically about an argument and to express in writing your position on that argument are being measured. You are not being evaluated on the position you take with respect to the argument.

The Analysis of an Issue Section

You will be presented with an issue and required to develop a position with respect to that issue. Specifically, the instructions will direct you to analyze that issue and to then present your views and perspectives on it.

There are four primary criteria on which your response will be evaluated. The first is the degree to which you have developed your position on the issue through the use of reasons and examples. Crucial here are the reasons and examples and the way in which they are interwoven in your position. The second is the degree of organization that your written response exhibits, ranging from well organized to totally disorganized. Taken together, these two criteria demand that you spend the first few (no more than five) minutes constructing a very brief outline of your response prior to beginning to write down your thoughts.

The third and fourth scoring criteria evaluate the manner in which you express your thoughts. The third is your facility with the written word—word choice, distinctiveness and use of words (diction), syntax (the flow of words within phrases and sentences), and variety of sentence structure. The fourth is the structure of your sentences and your adherence to the rules and guidelines of proper English (grammar).

Strategy

A strategy for attacking both essay questions is found at the end of this section. Here we will focus on a basic approach to attack the issues essay.

The general outline for your response is provided by the four criteria just described. In your initial paragraph you should clearly state the position that you are taking and make a general statement about the directions your second and third paragraphs will take. The second and third paragraphs should then contain the reasons, examples, and evidence that support your position. A third paragraph can introduce possible improvements to the situation being discussed. The fourth, which is recommended to be your final paragraph, should then summarize the positions you have taken and conclude your essay.

The Analysis of an Argument Section

The first characteristic evaluated will be your identification and analysis of the argument as presented. Important here is the clear and concise identification of the primary issue and the identification of the important features or characteristics of that issue. The second criterion is that your response be organized and flow well. You will also be evaluated on the degree to which your statements (and the points you make) support your main points.

To this core evaluation are added the same English-based criteria utilized in the issues section. Your diction, syntax, and sentence variety comprise one set of criteria. Your grammar, word usage, and structure comprise the second.

Strategy

The first paragraph calls for your identification of the main argument and the major points inherent in that argument. Included in these major points would be the assumptions and premises, explicit and implicit, that are inherent in the argument as presented. Both the argument and the assumptions and premises, then, should be the focus of your first paragraph.

Three paragraphs of text are then suggested. The first two can follow the pattern suggested for the issues section and contain your thoughts on the issues presented in the argument. Each paragraph should contain a thesis statement and at least two and no more than three points supporting your position. The last sentence of each paragraph should contain a transition sentence. Your third paragraph should focus on the way in which the argument, as presented, could be improved. You should end with a paragraph that summarizes what you have said and concludes your essay.

Common Essay Strategies: Your Real Opinion Does Not Matter

The position you take does not matter; how well you convey your position in writing does. It will likely be easier for you to adopt a position with which you are comfortable, but you may not be presented with an issue to which you have previously given a great deal of thought. If the issue is familiar, then take the stand you've already adopted. If it's not, then adopt whichever position is the easiest to develop within the suggested structure, regardless of whether it is the position you would normally take. It is the quality of writing that your essay portrays that is the basis for your score, not the position you take.

Some Thoughts About Your Reader

The bulk of the reading pool will have studied English extensively at the university level. This may be one of the ironies of the essays.

Good business English is not the same as good literary English. Good business English will meet the basic criteria of literary English, but the two are not the same. Both require a subject and a verb for a complete sentence and have other common, basic requirements, but business English tends to be terse and sharply focused, utilizing the minimum number of words to get the job done. Many styles of traditional English literature prefer longer sentences with vivid descriptors that contribute to the imagery of the sentence.

It is your objective to impress the reader in order to earn the highest possible score. Therefore, if there is an analogy from any literature you have read that you can work into your essay, it might work in your favor in the evaluation process. It will suggest that you are educated and well-read, a creative, integrative thinker.

Determine Your Typing Speed

The only way to determine how fast you can input words is to actually time yourself for the twenty minutes you should plan on allotting for the writing of your essay responses. (You should plan to use the first five minutes or less to outline your response and the last five to edit your response.) Your goal should be to conceptualize and type a minimum of sixteen to twenty quality sentences in the twenty minutes remaining.

Specific Essay-Writing Guidelines

Plan on writing the four to five paragraphs for each of the two topics in approximately twenty sentences. The first paragraph should be an introductory one in which you state your position, provide two to three sentences establishing the direction your second and third (and possibly fourth) paragraphs are going to take, and conclude with a transition sentence. Essentially, you will tell the reader what your position is and then introduce the reader to what you are going to say about your position in the subsequent paragraphs. If you should then happen to not complete your written response, you will still have the opportunity to earn some points for organization—the evaluator will at least know what you would have written had you not run out of time. Also, you may be able to get some credit for content.

Provide at least two paragraphs between the introductory and concluding paragraphs. These are the text or body paragraphs. In each, you will state a central thesis, present at least two sentences supporting your thesis statement, and close with a transition sentence to the next paragraph. If you can provide a third paragraph supporting your point, so much the better for your score. Don't try to incorporate a third point into the second paragraph if doing so keeps you from completing the third paragraph. You'll get more points by completing the third paragraph.

Developing an Outline

It is emphatically recommended that you prepare a very brief outline prior to beginning to write. One of the biggest mistakes you can make is to arrogantly begin writing, thinking that your writing will just organize itself. If you actually do have your essay well organized in your mind, it will not take you very long to document it on the paper provided, using only key words and phrases. Time yourself, and do not take more than five minutes for this process.

There are two approaches to the outline process. One is simply to write down key words or phrases that capture the essence of the points you want to make in the order they come to mind, ignoring for the moment how they fit into your essay. Then review each of the notations, determining where it fits into your paragraph structure. You might mark your points with a 1 if they are to be included in the introductory paragraph, a 2 or a 3 for the second and third paragraphs, and a 4 for the closing paragraph. Determine whether those items that fall into the second and third paragraphs are main thesis points or supporting points. Another approach is to write down the four paragraph designators and then classify each point as it comes to mind into its appropriate paragraph.

You may find that some points do not appear to fit into the structure as you have outlined it. Should this occur, then check to see if you have the minimum requirements for each of the four paragraphs. If you do, ignore the points that don't fit; you have what you need for the job at hand, and that is all that matters. If you don't, see if you can come up with an encompassing phrase, such as "economic issue," "political issue," or "social issue," that will expand the number of topics that can be incorporated. Developing these generic yet meaningful terms or phrases that fit with the topic can form the basis for the thesis statements of your text paragraphs. If this strategy does not seem to be working, quickly divert your attention to discerning other points that will fit into your outline.

Beginning Your Written Response

The opening sentence in your introductory paragraph should succinctly state the position which you are going to take. The second and third sentences should then introduce the reader to the position statements that you are going to make in the body paragraphs. Imagine that you make your second sentence of the introduction read, "In the next paragraph (two, three) relevant economic considerations will be presented. Then in the third paragraph, the relevant political issues will be discussed." You can use, "The last paragraph then summarizes the salient points and concludes this essay" as the closer to your introductory paragraph. (You can use this for both essays because the chances of both essays being read and remembered by the same individual are almost nil. Readers most assuredly will be assigned to specific questions in order to increase the likelihood of making consistent evaluations and to maximize efficiency.) In summary, your opening paragraph will contain a sentence stating your position, two to three sentences stating the direction your text paragraphs will take, and a transition statement.

Paragraphs two and three should also be at least four sentences in length. Each should begin with a general thesis statement. Your points supporting your position will then naturally follow. In your practice essays, you may find it rather easy to add two or three more sentences expanding upon your supporting statements. If so and if your typing speed can handle them, use them. Do not fall to the temptation to add more than three sentences, even if you know exactly what you are going to say. Adding more sentences than this may stop you from fully completing the essay. If possible and natural, try to use at least one compound sentence in either the second or third paragraphs. This should get you some added points for sentence structure and variety.

To summarize, you are looking at a basic four-sentence structure to each paragraph which can be modified and expanded as your situation and typing speed permit. This same guideline applies to the last, or concluding, paragraph in which you summarize the justification for the position you have taken.

Allot Five Minutes for Editing

Reserve the final five minutes for editing your essay. In the editing process you should do the following:

1. Review the structure of each sentence. Is each sentence a complete sentence? Does it have a subject and a verb?

2. Review the wording in your sentences. Are the tenses in agreement? Are the singular and plural in agreement?

3. Review your use of adjectives and adverbs. Are they correctly used?

4. Look for places where adjectives and adverbs can be added. If found, add no more than one or two. Adding some flair to your writing should get you added credit.

5. Check to see if you have used the same words repeatedly and/or within the vicinity of one another. If so, save time by developing a substitute phrase and judiciously inserting it into one or two places.

6. Check your spelling. The spell-check feature is not available.

One last thing: Verify that you have fully addressed the question which was asked.

International Students, Beware!

It is extremely important—in fact, required—that you practice writing your thoughts in English on the computer. Students for whom English is a foreign language are at a distinct disadvantage in the AWA sections. You have focused on developing your speaking skills, your comprehension skills, and your ability to write in the language, but how much time have you spent expressing your thoughts in English using a computer keyboard?

Lack of keyboard practice may put you at a great disadvantage and result in a much lower score than is reflective of your true ability. Practice your English input ability each day as part of your preparation process.

Two Weeks Preceding Test Day

You have worked hard for approximately two months. You have a good feel for the sections of the GMAT. You know where your strengths and weaknesses lie, and your timing has vastly improved. What can you do in the last two weeks before the test date? There is plenty you can do to hone your timing, fine-tune your techniques, and, most important, solidify your self-confidence and test-taking competence.

Now is the time to start taking the practice exams. As you go through these tests, be very strict with your timing, and try to simulate "battle conditions"—go from section to section without stopping. Take only the five-minute break allowed after the analytical writing and the quantitative sections. If possible, take at least one practice test at nine in the morning on the Saturday two weeks prior to the actual test. You'll be surprised at the difference time of day makes on your performance. If you're like most prospective MBAs, you'll have studied only at night. Your mind is much fresher in the morning, and you may be pleasantly surprised at your increased scoring performance. Remember, you're trying only to hone your test-taking skills in order to maximize your score. By now you realize that the GMAT is an analytical test, not a test of recall and knowledge.

On Friday evening you should review each of the exam sections and the strategies you have developed for attacking them. For example, for Reading Comprehension, you may want to review the six types of questions—main idea, facts, inference, logic, extrapolation, and tone. Then review your strategies for recognizing and selecting answers for each type of question. Do this for each of the exam segments.

During the day on Saturday, take one of the sample GMAT exams. On your first run, skip the AWA sections. At this point, there are two objectives. The first is to duplicate exam conditions as closely as possible, particularly with respect to the time allotted for each multiple-choice section. The second is to view this first run as a learning experience. Do not view your performance as an indication of how you are going to perform on test day.

On either Saturday evening or Sunday afternoon, grade the exam and review your performance on each section. Look at the questions you did not answer. Were they as difficult as they seemed, or could you, with a little more care, have correctly interpreted and answered them? Did you not answer them because of time? If so, is there any way that you can improve your speed? What questions did you miss? Why did you miss them? Were there techniques and approaches that you either forgot or neglected to use? Finally, look at your overall performance. What sections indicated a high level of achievement? Congratulate yourself on those. Which ones indicate that there is work to be done?

You have now determined your strategy and schedule for the remainder of the coming week. Study those sections for which additional work is indicated, starting with the most troublesome. Concentrate on only one section on any particular evening. This will enable you to concentrate on the problems, issues, and strategies relating to that section.

One Week Preceding Test Day

If you have done your work during the week, then seriously consider taking Friday night off and having some fun. Then on Saturday, preferably at 9:00 A.M., start your second practice GMAT. This time you should also do the AWA section. Again simulate the allotted exam times. Grade and review the multiple-choice sections on Saturday evening or early Sunday. Evaluate your writing sections as objectively as possible with emphasis on your ability to meet or exceed the minimum requirements suggested in this chapter. Review and evaluate the multiple-choice sections in the same manner as you did the previous week. Then, during the time remaining on Sunday, either take the third GMAT or simply take those sections with which you still feel uncomfortable. Review your performance on Monday evening. Use Tuesday and Wednesday to take your last shots at the remaining problem areas, using that fourth GMAT to tackle only these areas one last time. Do not try to do the complete exam at this point. Instead, generate as much free time, fun time, and rest time as possible.

Stop all of your GMAT work at least two days before you intend to take the exam in order to give your brain a good rest before the actual test. You will risk burnout unless you take this advice. If you study after this point it is likely you will find something that you have never seen before in your practice, and this will throw you psychologically.

Try to do as little as possible until the day on which you take the exam. If you can take the day before off, do it—be as "brainless" and relaxed as you can be. On the evening before the test, get together everything you will want to take with you: your GMAT ticket and at least one form of picture identification. There is no need for a watch because the computer will display the time, but take one if you so prefer (do not take a beeper watch or a calculator watch—they're not allowed). Do not take a listening device with headphones because these are not allowed. Earplugs are technically not allowed, but if you need quiet, the proctors may allow them.

Don't stay out late on the evening before test day. Go to sleep early and set your alarm so you can take a leisurely trip to the exam site.

Test Day

On test day, have a good breakfast to provide energy for the rather exhausting morning or afternoon that is ahead of you. Allow sufficient time to familiarize yourself with the computer and the computerized instructions. Take the test just as you have been doing all along. You won't see anything new or different, and if you have prepared adequately, you'll do just fine. That's all there is to maxing the GMAT!

A Final Thought

If you think of this test as a matching of wits, a game with the test maker, the test preparation will be a fun process. If you think about it for a minute, that's all it really is! There is no one at ETS who's any smarter than you are, and all the people there have done is written some questions, supplied you with the answers, and tried to distract you from finding the answer they want you to find. Have fun with the GMAT, and you'll do very well. When you leave the test site, you will know your score on the two multiple-choice sections, you can feel good about your performance, and you can breathe a big sigh of relief knowing that your results will be good for the next five years.

11
The Interview

Interviewing was initially discussed in Chapter 6. There the focus was split between how the interview is becoming a part of the admissions process and how to use the interview as an important part of the program evaluation and selection process. The focus of this chapter is on interviewing as a formal part of the admissions process. The objective is to increase your chances of being admitted to the program of your choice. Interviewing in this context can be approached using the guidelines and suggestions provided in the essay preparation chapters—look upon the interview as a form of spoken essay response.

Some schools are now requiring interviews as part of their selection process. Others encourage but do not require them. Many do not use them as part of their admissions process but instead provide them as part of their recruiting process when requested by applicants.

Should You Seek an Interview Even If It's Not Required?

People seek interviews for several reasons. Some feel that they interview well and that verbal communications skills are one of their strongest assets. If that's the case, an interview will probably strengthen their chances of admission. Another reason an applicant might arrange an interview, and a much more pragmatic one, is to influence the admissions committee in the event that he or she is put on the waiting list for admission. A final reason might be to seek information about the school—to find out firsthand if the school is the right choice. If all you seek is information, any representative of the school should be able to provide it. However, if your purpose is to advance the case for your admission, then you should attempt to speak with an admissions staff member. If you are traveling a long distance, it is especially important to make sure you will speak with a committee member. Some of the schools now requiring interviews use recent graduates or second-year students as assistant interviewers. Take the initiative and also request to speak with a committee member.

Types of Interviews

There are three basic types of interviews: on-campus, off-campus, and telephone. In an on-campus interview, you are much more likely to be speaking with a member of the admissions staff. This type should be your preference, if you are given a choice, because it is much more likely to advance your case.

Off-campus interviews are generally conducted by an alumnus of the school who lives and works in your area. The interview will be more relaxed (probably over lunch or dinner), and you will find that you may have more in common with this type of interviewer. One potential drawback is that you cannot be sure of the weight that this type of interview will carry in comparison with an on-campus interview. You can be assured, however, that the alum's comments will be read and considered; some alumni can be quite influential if they are well connected to the school.

The third type, the telephone interview, is available to international students and to U.S. applicants who live a long distance from the campus and in areas without alumni or areas to which admissions officers are not able to travel. These types of interviews are quite effective in the selection process and should be taken seriously. These interviews are often conducted by the business school's staff and/or specially selected students, people who will play an influential role in the process.

How to Prepare for the Interview

Whichever type of interview is available to you, set up your own agenda. Remember that the interview should be used to introduce new material, not to rehash information already available on the application. You might take three sheets of paper and head them, Major Theme, New Evidence, and General Impression. On the first sheet, state as succinctly as possible the one idea you wish to leave in the interviewer's mind after the session. On the second sheet, put down the material that will support the theme and that you hope to work into the conversation. The general impression is harder to pinpoint. Ask yourself, at your best, how do people perceive you? Are you quiet and determined? Outgoing? A numbers person? People oriented? Obviously, your personality contains many of these disparate elements, but in a short interview you cannot convey every facet of your character. Select what you think are your best assets, and try to get those aspects of your nature across. Work to control the interview; don't let yourself be controlled by it.

Prepare yourself to meet different types of interviewers. In general, you will meet well-trained, professional people, but occasionally you will find someone who is less experienced, less trained, or less capable. Whatever the situation, you have to play it to the best of your ability. Sometimes an interviewer will use ploys that could create problems for you. One of these might be a series of rapid-fire questions, a tactic designed to put you off guard. Interviewers do this to see how you react under stressful conditions. The key to handling this type of situation is to try not to lose your composure. If you have done your homework, you will know how to answer most of the questions thrown at you; if you don't know an answer, say so. Consider countering by complimenting the interviewer on the quality or creativity of the question by admitting that you had never thought of that, and ask the interviewer for his or her thoughts on the question. Take the initiative when the opportunity occurs by asking a question of your own. Never forget your basic theme. Try to work your theme and evidence into the conversation as much as possible. In this case, what you say is not as important as conveying the impression that you are able to stay cool under pressure and to perform in an impressive, if not brilliant, fashion.

Another trick to prepare for is the use of chatty informality. Interviewers who chat about the weather, sports, and anything seemingly aimless are trying to find out whether you can take control of a situation. Here again, your job is to get across the basic theme and evidence that you planned to present. You must bring the conversation back to topics that will enhance your chances for admission and enable you to show why you would make an ideal candidate. If you are not prepared, you will not be able to take constructive control, and the interview will have been wasted and perhaps counterproductive.

If you are really motivated and you want to be thoroughly prepared, then you should seriously consider doing a mock interview. This is an excellent way to prepare. Have a friend play the role of the interviewer or rehearse in front of a mirror. The mirror is very effective for observing nonverbal behavior (you can examine posture, hands, eye contact), while the role-playing will give you the benefit of another person's reaction to your answers, behavior, and demeanor. You might want to try simply preparing some questions and answering them into a tape recorder. This is especially beneficial for judging your verbal presentation. Do you speak cogently on a given question or is your response a series of "umms"? Do you speak slowly and distinctly so that the interviewer can understand and appreciate what you are saying? Or do you talk at the speed of light in order to get through the question? Are you satisfied with your response? Are you satisfied with your presentation style?

Whatever you do, don't repeat yourself, and don't repeat the catalog. The interviewer will most likely have read or been told the contents of your application and will expect that you have read the catalog. If you ask questions that are already answered in the catalog or if you volunteer information already covered in depth in your application, you may do more harm than good. However, asking questions to clarify statements made in the program literature is acceptable. Nevertheless, you should always have a current resume with you in case the interviewer has not read your application. Always review your application and essays before the interview.

Throughout, you must keep in mind the objective of the interview and of the interview process—so the school can find out something about you that is not evident in your application. Doesn't that theme sound familiar? Isn't this the constant theme of the essays? After reviewing some interviewing guidelines, we'll return to this essay-interview connection.

Some Interviewing Guidelines

First, be conscious of how you look. Dress conservatively. Do not take this opportunity to wear trendy clothing. Be well groomed. Your goal is to make an impression through your verbal interaction, not through your stylish dress. Treat the interview as a job interview.

Second, be aware of body language. Strive to maintain eye contact with your interviewer as this exudes confidence and helps establish rapport. It's a signal to your interviewer that you are a mature, well-adjusted, confident person. Shake hands firmly with your interviewer, both upon greeting and upon parting, as this too suggests self-confidence and an ability to handle professional situations. Do not overdo it, though; "meatgrinder" handshakes that go on for a long time are not appropriate. Maintain good posture and don't fidget, hide your mouth behind your fingers or hand, or play with your hair or nails. You do not want to come across as nervous or lacking in social graces.

Third, strive to communicate positive personal characteristics. In other words, arrive slightly early, show respect and courtesy, exude energy and enthusiasm, end the interview on a positive note, and send a thank-you note shortly after the interview is over. Sending a note shows good manners and thoughtfulness and leaves a positive impression on the interviewer. The note can be handwritten or typed, although handwritten is more socially correct and more personal, and can be very brief: "Dear XYZ: Thank you for your time last Friday afternoon, October 22. It was a pleasure to speak with you. I appreciate the information that you gave me about___, and I look forward to hearing from the committee. Sincerely, Frank Lee Hopeful." If your handwriting is poor, then type the note. In this electronic age of communications, saying thank you via e-mail is becoming acceptable.

Keep the following rules in mind:

1. Do not under any circumstances smoke, tell jokes, respond in an arrogant manner, eat or drink during the interview, make patronizing or personal remarks about your interviewer, or

argue with the interviewer. Becoming too familiar ultimately shows a lack of respect.

2. Even if the interviewer offers you something to drink, such as a cup of coffee, politely refuse. It's simply not appropriate, even if the interviewer is drinking. Props like cigarettes and coffee cups will detract from your presentation.

3. Remember, you are there to make an impression, not to entertain. A light quip is fine, and properly displaying your sense of humor will positively add to your image, but don't ever risk telling jokes that might offend your interviewer. Laughing at a joke is fine but don't feel you need to respond in kind.

4. Respond carefully. You may be faced with an interviewer who insists upon bringing up controversial topics to play devil's advocate. This interviewer is trying to test either your reasoning skills and/or your ability to maintain your composure under pressure. Defend your position objectively rather than argumentatively. Never allow the discussion to become a confrontation.

5. Be careful of arrogance. It's one thing to be self-confident and self-assured, and another to be arrogant. It's a fine line to walk, because you'll be tooting your own horn. Stress your positive qualities and accomplishments, but do not appear to think yourself superior to either the interviewer or to most other candidates.

The Kinds of Questions to Expect

The kinds of questions you might be asked during an interview range from those that could just as easily have appeared in the essay section of an application to very straightforward questions. No matter how they strike you, just remember that all are designed and intended to help the interviewer learn more about you. Consider the following two questions:

Tell me something about yourself.

What else would you like the admissions committee to know about you that has not been covered in your application?

These are commonly asked questions, so you must be ready for them. Prepare in the fashion discussed in the essay chapters. They can be challenging because they are so vague, and they can catch the unprepared off guard. What should you say? What should you omit? What does the interviewer want to know?

Use the opportunity provided by these questions to summarize your positive qualities and to convey your major theme and general impression. This is your chance to broaden and deepen the interviewer's knowledge of you. If you have prepared with the self-marketing strategy suggested at the beginning of this chapter, then you are in a prime position and ready to take control. Remember, this is a marketing situation, so sell yourself!

Now consider the following questions. These have a more specific focus—your job environment—but they are still intended to find out more about the unique you:

How did you get your current job?

How would you describe your current job and what do you like and dislike about it?

Describe your ideal work environment and your role within that environment.

How have you been particularly effective as a team member?

Although the thrust of these questions might initially take you by surprise, a quick read of the intent will take you directly to the basic three-point strategy of how your experience has influenced who you are today, how your experiences within the context of the question have helped to shape your career plan, and why you want to pursue the MBA now. Chances are that you will have considered the concepts inherent in these questions as part of the application process and that you will find yourself prepared for these types of questions.

Some of the questions could just as easily focus on you as an individual rather than on you as an employee:

Share a personal or professional obstacle you have faced. How did you overcome this obstacle?

How are you motivated? Describe a situation that illustrates that you were motivated.

Describe one of your most challenging encounters. How did you respond to this encounter and what did you learn from the experience?

Describe a situation in which you had to resolve a conflict. What did you learn from this experience?

Take a few seconds to gather your thoughts using this three-step approach. Briefly describe the situation, experience, or encounter. Then describe what you learned from it. Again, where applicable, show how this has helped to influence your decision to pursue the MBA.

What happens if someone asks you,

What other schools are you applying to?

Watch out! This question, innocent as it may seem, has some potential pitfalls. As has been stressed throughout this book, answer honestly, but don't run off a list of twenty schools running the gamut from the top five to the totally undistinguished and unknown. Instead, mention those three or four schools that you have every intention of attending if you are accepted. If the schools mentioned are roughly on par with the school asking the question, then you are in relatively good shape. If there is a wide disparity, problems may arise. You run the risk, for example, of making it seem that the interviewing school will be a consolation prize if you are not admitted to a much more prestigious school. You may also run a risk if your list conveys that the interviewing school is your "reach" or "dream" school. The true implications will be as varied as the individuals asking the question, which means that there is no right answer—only an honest one. Your objective is to subtly let the interviewer know that your intent is to attend one of the mentioned schools.

At this point the types of questions should be sounding quite similar to the essay categories presented and discussed in Chapter 8. Recall that one of the categories was Creative Brainbenders. Consider the following questions:

Who are your heroes, contemporary or historical?

If you could spend time with any person—living, dead, or fictional—whom would you select, and why?

If you had a chance to eat dinner with any distinguished person of your choice, who would that person be?

This type of question is tough because it can catch you off guard, but it is effective because it allows for individuality. You will be remembered for your choice, so make it a good one. Interpret the word *hero* loosely—it doesn't have to be someone famous. It doesn't have to be a business leader. Your choice will say a lot about who you are, so take your time and think long and hard about who you would really want to spend time with or who you really admire and why.

Consider, for example, the following questions, which are offshoots of the For Fun application essay question category:

> What book have you read that is of great significance to you?
> What is your favorite book and why?
> What section of a bookstore do you head for first?
> What magazines and/or newspapers do you read regularly?
> What is your favorite movie or TV show?

This type of question also allows for much individuality, and you should welcome the chance to set yourself apart from the competition. These questions are designed to find out a bit more about the habits, hobbies, and interests that weren't covered in the application. Do not repeat anything you might have mentioned in your essays. Steer clear of answers that could be questionable in logic—be honest about your choices and be prepared to discuss the authors of books, and the formats of magazines and newspapers. Be aware of the thrust and theme of a publication, be it political or literary in nature. Be prepared to discuss your choice of television show or movie—why is it your favorite?

Another type of question deals with current affairs or controversial issues:

> Describe a national or international issue of concern to you. Why does it concern you?
>
> How do you feel about an issue in current events: nuclear testing, abortion, drugs, gun control, etc.?
>
> What is the world's biggest problem, and what do you advocate for its solution?

Be prepared to talk about current issues in the news. The most formidable part of these questions is selecting the issue. Use your colleagues and friends as sounding boards. Watch Sunday morning debate programs, ABC's "Nightline," "48 Hours" on CBS, or other programs covering important topics and events. If you faithfully read newspapers, then you should have a basic handle on the issues that will likely arise for discussion purposes. If you are knowledgeable about a specific area, this is the time to exhibit your competence. It is important for you to have well-thought-out points of view about the world around you. This is crucial, because it shows that you are a mature, aware, and socially conscious person. Defend your points of view with logical arguments. These questions will allow you the opportunity to assert your individuality and intelligence. Welcome the opportunity to express yourself. Remember that it is your awareness of an issue, not the position you take with respect to the issue, that is important.

As a final part of the interview, you may be asked if you have any questions about the school or the program. Even if you are not asked, make sure that you have two or three good questions ready and ask them. This will show that you have done your homework and have a true interest in the program. Make sure the questions are not covered in the catalog, but choose questions that can be answered by the interviewer—don't play "stump the interviewer." Examples of questions are: "Will you be adding any new majors, courses, professors, programs, or clubs?" "What are the opportunities for employment while at school?" and "Are you expecting any changes in recruiting this year?" For others, review the section on interviews in Chapter 6.

Conclusion

The interview can be helpful or harmful to you, depending on your preparation and verbal communication abilities. If you are of the opinion that you can more effectively and impressively present yourself in person than on paper, then you should welcome the chance to interview. If you follow the guidelines in this chapter, your interviews have every chance of being highly successful.

Responding to the Schools' Responses

Do not read this chapter until you have completed all of your applications, interviews, and have heard from at least one school. With a bit of luck, you will be accepted to a school of your choice. Once you are, it's decision-making time.

Accepting an Offer of Admission

The first action you must take is to make a nonrefundable tuition deposit. Most schools require that such a deposit accompany an acceptance. Make sure before you accept an offer of admission that you really want to go to that school. If you haven't heard from your top-choice school, try to delay responding and making a deposit for as long as possible. If you are forced to make a choice, then pick your next-best choice and send in your deposit. The MBA application process has been an expensive one. If you get accepted to your first-choice school at a later date, you can forfeit the deposit to the second-choice school and just think of it as another MBA application investment. At least that way you will be assured of a place in one of the schools to which you applied.

In the best of all possible worlds, you will be accepted at all the schools to which you applied. Then, if you are still undecided, you might want to think about the costs of each school. If one school offers you a better financial aid package than another, perhaps that is where you should go—provided, of course, that the schools are equal in reputation and that the anticipated quality of your experience will be the same.

Reputation should be the first test you apply in making the final choice. Obviously, most people go to the best school they can get into. Given the number of schools with national reputations, program culture, cost, and location are the next factors that you should consider. Of these, cost usually gets top billing. Pay some very close attention, however, to your instincts concerning culture. To make the final decision, carefully review the key criteria that you used to develop your application list: teaching methodology; placement success in your area of interest; and program location. While attending the most highly regarded program might be worth your investment, it might be better in the long run to attend a well-regarded (but less highly ranked) program that provides scholarship support and has a record of success in your intended career field. You will be making a huge investment in time and money. You should be comfortable with the anticipated return on your investment.

The Waiting List

The *waiting list* and the *wasteland* are synonymous in the mind of most applicants. You have not been accepted. You have not been rejected. At least, you have received a signal that the institution has some highly positive perspectives of you. If your first-choice institution places you on its waiting list, your level of anxiety and frustration will rise to an even higher level—so close yet so far. What can and should you do in this situation?

Your first impulse will be to call the admissions staff in order to determine whether there is any action you can take to change that decision to acceptance. You have the right to do this, but before you do, be aware of the following considerations. Extremely busy admissions staff are frequently inundated with calls for numerous types of inquiries. If you have specific questions that need answering, then go ahead and call the office. Be respectful and be sensitive to the volume of their work. Asking questions usually does not hurt your chances because admissions staffs are so accustomed to these questions. However, should you become a pest by continuing to call and push the issue, you could anger the admissions staff. Accordingly, it is better to write a letter than to call.

There are two questions that you have every right to ask and one action step you can take as a member of the waiting list. First, you can inquire about your position on the wait list. That is, are you first, tenth, or twentieth? Some schools do not rank order the applicants on their waiting list. Second, you can inquire about the number of people on the list who are, on average, offered admission each year. Obtaining this information enables you to estimate the likelihood of your being admitted. The action step you can then take is to sincerely thank the admissions representative for the information, explaining that the university is your top choice, and expressing your hope that you have the opportunity to become a part of the incoming class.

Here are some additional suggestions:

- Be sure to respond immediately and in writing, stating your interest in remaining on the waiting list.

- Add one to two additional reasons not expressed in your application stating why you would be an asset to the program and why you specifically want to attend that school.

- Do not badger the admissions staff, the receptionist, or the committee members with too many phone calls or with too many letters.

- Inquire whether an additional letter of recommendation would benefit your cause.

The most legitimate reason for contacting the school is to communicate something significant that has happened that has every chance of impressing upon the admissions staff that you are, without a doubt, a person that "must" be admitted. Two common events that fall into this category are receiving a promotion and receiving some honor or recognition. These are legitimate and significant types of information that reflect characteristics every program is seeking and that all admissions staff members would like to have brought to their attention.

There is a saying—"on the waiting list this year, accepted next." On the surface, this makes some sense in that if your strengths were sufficiently strong to at least get you on the list, then your accomplishments over the next year should make you an even stronger candidate. The downside to this reasoning is that there will be a new group of applicants next year against whom you will once again have to compete. There is always the chance that next year's applicant pool will contain a larger number of even more competitive applications, particularly if some highly positive school news has appeared in the national press or a major move in the school's perceived ranking has occurred. High quality, competitive programs have been encountering rapid increases (30 percent or more) in the size of their applicant pools rather consistently in recent years. Therefore, one cannot assume that being wait-listed one year will mean automatic acceptance next year.

Our most important advice is this: If a particular program is definitely your top choice, if the strength of your commitment to the program is so strong that you are willing to forego your current admission to other programs in order to reapply to your top choice next year, and if you truly feel that you can make yourself more competitive in the selection process, then you have an obligation to yourself to do so. In weighing the pros and cons of this decision, you must carefully and realistically consider your situation. If the wait list program is a definite "stretch," and you are reacting to your competitive nature rather than recognizing that there are other programs that are equally or better suited for you, then you definitely need to critically reevaluate your answers to "Why the MBA?" and "Why now?"

If You Are Not Accepted

The decision among several offers of admission is difficult, but as decisions go, it's a nice one to be able to make. The more painful decision is about what to do if you are rejected by the MBA programs you feel are best for you. Counting yourself out of the picture is not an option. Instead, contact the admissions staff and ask how your personal profile and application need to be improved in order to significantly enhance your chances of being accepted. Determine why you were not accepted, correct the problem, and reapply.

As you again begin the application process, it is important that you not make the same mistakes twice. As indicated, your first step should be to try to find out why you were rejected. Quite often a friendly admissions staff member will tell you the reasons for your rejection. If you cannot find out, read this book again very carefully with your applications in hand. Weigh the advice given against what you see on your application as objectively as you can, or get someone else to do it for you. Are any discrepancies evident? It may be that you didn't adhere to word limits, for instance, or that you weren't sufficiently specific in supporting your assertions. Perhaps you did not adequately prepare for the GMAT and so your test scores are less than competitive for your program of choice.

It may be that you simply applied too soon. Not having sufficient practical business experience is a common reason for rejection at the competitive schools. The solution to this problem is quite easy: Wait a year or two and reapply. If you are stuck in a routine job that you cannot leave, then volunteer for an interesting community service project. You already know the type of experience the competitive MBA programs are looking for, so get involved in work that will give you that experience.

If you conclude that you were rejected because of a poor undergraduate record or low GMAT scores, then enroll in some part-time graduate courses, especially in business-related courses. It is imperative that you demonstrate your quantitative competence and your communications skills. If there is some question about your abilities in either of these two areas, then consider enrolling in a quantitative preparation course, a speech course, an English writing course, or an English course that requires extensive reading. These same recommendations are applicable to international students who may have demonstrated the need to improve their writing skills, listening comprehension, or language fluency. The strong grades you earn will help convince the admissions committee that your undergraduate grades no longer represent either your current level of ability or your future level of achievement. Note that by taking the educational initiatives just mentioned, you will also be preparing yourself to retake the GMAT should that be necessary.

Alternatively, your rejection by competitive programs may have hinged on your work experience and how you presented yourself in the essays. If so, this might be a good time to reevaluate your current situation. Are there opportunities for you to assume more authority and responsibility in your present job? Are there more creative approaches you could use in problem solving? Can you tighten up your essays? If the answer is yes, then do it—you owe it to yourself.

Your second option, of course, is to reassess your characteristics and apply to schools that more closely reflect your profile and that offer a better chance for acceptance. Not getting an MBA is not an option for readers of this book. All of the recommendations made in this book are based on the assumption that you are committed to an MBA career path. If the MBA was right for you when you started the application process, then it is right for you now.

Concluding Thoughts

It is hoped that this book has been helpful to you in your quest to gain acceptance to the selective MBA program of your choice, because that was its goal. Chances are better than good that you have been accepted to one of your choice schools by this point. If so, congratulations! You're off to an exciting and rewarding experience. If not, don't give up—reread this book, begin your preparation, and try your hand again. Believe in it and go for it!

Appendix

Relevant Reference Material

It is recommended that you be particularly careful when purchasing references on the process of preparing for the GMAT. A major change occurred in 1997 when the GMAC implemented CAT (Computer Adaptive Testing). Use only study guides published since that time.

Highly Recommended

The Official Guide for GMAT Review, 9th ed. Graduate Management Admissions Council, 1997.

GMAT: POWERPREP Software. Graduate Management Admissions Council, 1997.

The Official Guide to MBA Programs, 9th ed. Graduate Management Admissions Council, 1997.

Other GMAT Preparation Sources

Arco GMAT Supercourse, 6th ed. MacMillan, 1997.

Barron's How to Prepare for the GMAT, 11th ed. Eugene D. Jaffe and Stephen Hilbert. Barron's, 1998.

Cliffs GMAT CAT. Jerry Bobrow. Cliffs Notes, 1997.

GMAT CAT. Research & Education Association, 1998.

The GMAT for DUMMIES. Suzee Vlk. IDG Books Worldwide, 1998.

Kaplan GMAT 1997–1998. Simon & Schuster, 1997.

The Princeton Review, GMAT CAT, 1998. Geoff Martz. Princeton Review Publishing, 1998.

On MBA Programs

A Business Week Guide—The Best Business Schools, 5th ed. John A. Byrne. McGraw-Hill, Inc., 1997.

Barron's Guide to Graduate Business Schools, 10th ed. Barron's Educational Series, Inc., 1997.

Which MBA? 8th ed. George Bickerstaffe. Addison-Wesley, 1997.

Application Software

College EDGE. 101 Townsend, Suite 333, San Francisco, CA 94107. http://www.MBA.CollegeEdge.com. Phone: 415-778-6262.

MBA MULTI-App. 740 South Chester Road, Suite F, Swarthmore, PA, 19801. Phone: 1-800-516-2227. mcs@multi-app.com.

Financing Your MBA

The Official Guide to Financing Your MBA, 1st ed. Bart Astor, ed. Graduate Management Admissions Council.